Servants Without Hire

Emerging Concepts of the Christian Ministry in the Campbell-Stone Movement

Servants Without Hire

Emerging Concepts of the Christian Ministry in the Campbell-Stone Movement

by

William Martin Smith

The Reed Lectures for 1967

(THIRD ANNUAL SERIES)

THE DISCIPLES OF CHRIST HISTORICAL SOCIETY

NASHVILLE, TENNESSEE

1968

Preface

The Forrest F. Reed Lectures were brilliantly inaugurated in November 1965, by Dr. W. Barnett Blakemore, Dean of the Disciples Divinity House, Chicago, Illinois.

The second series was delivered by three Lecturers who were asked to evaluate the religious scene both historically and currently from their respective positions within the Campbell-Stone Movement. Those delivering the Lectures were Dr. David Edwin Harrell, then of Johnson City, Tennessee; Dr. Robert O. Fife, Milligan College, Tennessee; and Dr. Ronald E. Osborn, Indianapolis, Indiana. The series continued the high level of performance established in 1965.

The Committee to plan for the 1967 Forrest F. Reed Lectures chose the theme "Emerging Concepts of the Christian Ministry in the Campbell-Stone Movement."

The invitation extended to Dr. William Martin Smith of Indianapolis, Indiana to deliver these Lectures stated:

It is our hope that the Lecturer . . . will discuss the historical, sociological and theological influences as well as interpret the present trends in the enlarging ministry.

Dr. Smith has complied admirably with the gigantic task requested of him. His scholarly research and his love and understanding of the Christian Ministry commend these

Lectures to the reader who in turn will become knowledgeable of the factors affecting the Christian Ministry as it has developed in the Campbell-Stone Movement.

HARRY M. DAVIS, *Chairman*

Louis Cochran
Willis R. Jones
Ronald E. Osborn
Forrest F. Reed
Hugh M. Riley

Foreword

The Forrest F. Reed Lectureship was established October 3, 1964, and is held annually under the auspices of the Disciples of Christ Historical Society. Funds for its endowment were given through a permanent trust created by Forrest F. Reed, Disciple layman of Nashville, Tennessee, and a member of the Board of Trustees of the Historical Society.

By specific request and unanimous action of the Board of Trustees, the Lectureship has been named in honor of its donor. Its purpose, as described in the trust agreement set up by Mr. Reed, is to provide "a series of lectures by history scholars objectively interpreting some phase of (Disciple) church history."

Forrest F. Reed was Chairman of the Nashville Planning Committee which brought the Disciples of Christ Historical Society to Nashville in 1952. He has been a member of the Board of Trustees since 1952, and was Chairman from July 1, 1962 through June 30, 1966. Mr. Reed is a former member of the Board of Directors of Unified Promotion, Indianapolis, Indiana; and a former member of the Board of Lexington Theological Seminary, Lexington, Kentucky. He is a charter member of Woodmont Christian Church in Nashville and for ten years was Chairman of the Board of Trustees of the Disciples Divinity House of Vanderbilt University. Mr. Reed has recently retired as President of the Tennessee Book Company, Nashville. He is President of Reed and Company, publishing firm in Nashville.

Dr. William Martin Smith is Vice-President of the Pension Fund of Christian Churches, Indianapolis, Indiana. Prior to coming to the staff of the Pension Fund in 1951 he spent sixteen years in the pastorate. He is author of the widely used book *For the Support of the Ministry*, and he has written many pamphlets and articles concerning the church, the ministry, and Christian stewardship. Dr. Smith's academic background includes the A. B. and M. A. degrees from Phillips University, the B. D. degree from the Graduate Seminary, Phillips University, the Th. M. from Christian Theological Seminary, and graduate studies at Teachers' College, Columbia University and Union Theological Seminary in New York. He is the recipient of the Doctor of Divinity degree from Christian Theological Seminary.

WILLIS R. JONES, president-curator
DISCIPLES OF CHRIST HISTORICAL SOCIETY

Contents

I

A Nineteenth Century Revolution

A Free Ministry in a Free Society

Recently I was, for a time, without my automobile. It was stolen, but soon recovered. Without it, I experienced an inconvenience, easily surpassed by any present day pastor facing the same crisis. For the American minister, transportation has *always* been critical. During the eighteen hundreds, the loss of certain horses would have set "The Nineteenth Century Reformation" back more than theological error. Those who early joined the Campbell-Stone group shared this one characteristic: *They were men on the move.*

There is more than one reason that, almost a century later, some should dub this emerging communion, "a movement." It was a restless time. East was moving west, and west was spreading itself all over a continually expanding territory. The old Gospel refrain of a century ago echoed the mobile rhythm of this group and the spirit of its kinetic ministry. It went—

> I am bound for the promised land,
> I am bound for the promised land;
> O, who will come and go with me,
> I am bound for the promised land.[1]

As the frontier singer drew out the word, "La-a-and," one could feel the swinging surge of horse and oxen. Sail, flatboat, prairie schooner and buckboard ultimately gave way to steam and steel, but they moved on, these ministers of the nineteenth century. This common mark affected how they saw themselves and how we should see them, too.

First, we should observe that they came from places with substantial historical backgrounds which conditioned their lives and thoughts, introducing the basic religious and social problems as they saw them.

Second, they came into something—a culture, a society, a totally new, fully American atmosphere that greatly modified everything they brought.

A careful analysis has not yet been made of just how they were conditioned by the seventeenth and eighteenth centuries. What study we have largely concerns their theological and philosophical backgrounds, and generally fails to consider the social, cultural, and political forces that shaped the Campbell-Stone Movement. These should not be neglected by us, nor deprecated. God worked in them then and works through them now. Past neglect may have arisen from such pre-occupation with theological and Biblical correctness, so as to obscure the basic forces that shaped our history.

I recall the "preaching charts" which my father and other preachers of the past generations used to trace the historical development of the Disciples of Christ. Not only were Luther, Calvin and Zwingli brought loosely into the picture, I am certain that the claimed relationships to Roger Williams, Elias Smith, Abner Jones and James O'Kelly were of such uncertain nature that these gentlemen would have been "shocked" to have been so directly included among our ancestors. Our historical case will fall if we pick antecedents only on the basis of what seems to us to have been doctrinal agreements but which are not established in fact.

What I hope to do here is to stimulate some desire to look at the cultural, social and economic forces that developed American society, and ask what effect they had in shaping the ministry of the Christian Church, particularly the Campbell-Stone Movement.

To begin with, most of its ancestors and originators came from Scotland and Northern Ireland. They were mainly Presbyterian. They came to this country with divisions that became quite irrelevant here, particularly after the war of Independence.

Most of our fathers were familiar with the troubles their forebears had experienced with the state church. Even though there had been religious peace at one time or another in Scotland, it was generally an enforced peace, under much "official" control. For the most part, the Presbyterians there exercised great patience, believing firmly that the "due process of law" would bring justice and rectify most wrongs. Only gradually did the idea dawn upon Scotch Presbyterians that the government had no business in running the religious affairs of the church. As this idea got hold of them, generally those most persuaded found it expedient to migrate to the colonies. Out of these ideological struggles as well as the hard, economic conditions in Scotland and Ireland, the Presbyterians and Independents came to these American shores—some as early as the seventeenth century, many others with the Campbells early in the nineteenth.

Both of the Campbells and Barton W. Stone were from this background. They were familiar with Richard Baxter's concepts of the ministry. He had striven for harmony between the Presbyterians, Episcopalians and Independents during the seventeenth century in Britain. He was a substantial scholar and a great pastor, and a non-conformist whose ideas became the seed out of which many American concepts of the church and its ministry arose. He wrote:

If God would reform the ministry and set them on their duties zealously and faithfully, the people would certainly be reformed. All churches, either rise or fall as far as the ministry doth rise or fall, not in riches or worldly grandeur, but in knowledge, zeal and ability of their work.[2]

A Presbyterian divine, by the interesting name of John Smith, died in Edinburgh in the very year in which Thomas Campbell left for America. His lectures[3] on the Christian ministry, made before the Synod of Argyl, follow many of Baxter's ideas. The Smith lectures were popular enough to be republished in America in 1812. Not too many things were being imported from England that year. It had to be an acceptable book. Of interest to me, is that my copy, now more than 150 years old, belonged to some of my ancestors who were with the Republican Methodists in Surrey County, Virginia at the turn of the nineteenth century. So Richard Baxter's and John Smith's concepts of the ministry found their way and had their impact in 1800 in America.

At that time a Revolutionary War was just coming to a close in America. Every school boy knows that. But he may not know there was also a revolution going on in the church. It had really started several centuries earlier. By 1809 it was taking shape and form in America. It centered on the ministry. It was a part of the continuing reformation of the church. All our early fathers recognized this.

Luther had broken the priestly hierarchy down and had emphasized the priesthood of all believers and that the clergy were a part of the laity, since the "laos" were the people of God. But Luther and Calvin believed in a *set-apart* public ministry. With Luther, the authority of the preacher centered in the Holy Spirit, with Calvin, in the Word of God. The effects of the sixteenth century Reformation (particularly stemming from Calvin) upon this "new world" have long been acknowledged. Their impact upon Campbell and Stone are just now being recognized.

While they may have rejected Calvin in soteriological doctrines of salvation, they very much followed him in ecclesiological concepts regarding the ministry. Like Calvin, they believed that there was a set-apart ministry, and that the ministry must be chosen with utmost care and should be fully trained, not merely in the Bible, but in all of those disciplines of the liberal arts and sciences which expanded the mind of man and made it possible for him to be sensitive and aware of his history and his community.

Nineteenth century America has often been caricaturized by its rugged individualism. In religion, Puritanism and individual piety have been emphasized as peculiar American traits. But one essential ingredient has often been overlooked, and that was the cry for *order* and *responsible personal relationships* in a democratic (but responsible) society. It is basic to the philosophies and theologies that gave birth to the American dream. And it is to this, that one might wish the Campbell-Stone Movement had been more successfully addressed.

The United States is too near its beginnings, even yet, to fully understand the influences that came largely from the Calvinists in France, Hungary, Holland and Scotland. It affected both Campbell and Stone and it affected America. It was here in the hills before the "shot was fired that was heard round the world." It was the climate into which our fathers began their preaching.

The anti-institutionalism of our present age could have scarcely matched that of the early nineteenth century. Our early ministers were determined not to be "bought" at any price. They had traversed the stormy seas, experienced the privations of war, exposed themselves to the dangers of the frontier in order to have a sort of freedom. They understood that ministry meant servanthood, but they were determined to be "servants without hire."

All of Mr. Campbell's early declarations against "a hireling clergy" are addressed to this. His ideas, however, are hard to fathom without knowing something of the state church in the eighteenth century and particularly how the ministry was involved. Every activity of the Scotch and British ministry from seminary to the grave carried the paternalism of government with it. Individuals were appointed because of family relationships. "Stipends" were set. Even this word, "stipend," which was frequently used in place of wage or salary, was probably an indication of guilt feelings that many had concerning the arrangement.

What provoked many a Scotchman was the publishing of "fees" at each place of worship. So much was charged for baptism, for prayers, weddings, funerals and the like. The government sponsored it all. Our early fathers were in revolt against this! Indeed, the revolt against George III was as much religious as political. Barton W. Stone declared, "From my earliest recollection I drank deeply into the spirit of liberty and was so warmed by the soul-inspiring draughts, that I could not hear the name of British or Tories, without feeling a rush of blood through my whole system."[4]

Even such a cool head as Alexander Campbell, not given to strident emotion, found himself genuinely stirred. He intended to attack the *abuse,* not the *use* of the ministry, in *The Christian Baptist.* But it was fresh in his mind that much of the sectarianism of his day had been government sponsored. That did it! The clergy he attacked and those that he distrusted so much were someway officially sponsored. Today we would call them a "status ministry." This period of his thought and writing, which is so obviously an over-reaction to the European scene, is still not understood historically by many. Even yet, some persons see Mr. Campbell as only truly alert in his *Christian Baptist* days. They allow little room for change. And regarding the ministry, change he did. That is hardly to be denied. True, his change on some matters is so subtle that many do not see it. Even Campbell himself probably would have argued, with much verbiage that his views were basically the same. But on the ministry, the radical changes are apparent not alone in what he said, but what he did.

Much of the religious revolution was occurring in Virginia. When the war closed, Virginia was the most populous colony. It had contributed largely to the winning of the

American independence both in soldiers and in money. Its statesmen and moral influence had been central in the forming of this republic. In the center of Virginia life had been the Episcopal church which still held some dominance, even though active membership was at an all time low. At the conclusion of the war, many ministers of this great communion left and returned to the homeland.

Back in the Virginia hills already were scores of families of Calvinistic background, both Baptist and Presbyterian. It was to, and through, these that Campbell and Stone were most effective. These people were rejoicing that the state church at last was finally dis-established. At the same time, it was a terribly hard time economically. People were literally living off the land.

On the very heels of the war a great westward movement began which beckoned many more settlers anxious to taste this new freedom. Kentucky was a wilderness. People poured into it from Virginia and the Carolinas. In less than twenty years, the Bluegrass State was populated.

Most were from Scotch and Irish stock. Many had landed on the Delaware, Virginia and Carolina beaches in the seventeenth century but had moved back toward the Blue Ridge and remained there for a hundred years or so, rarely crossing until the turn of the century. Many were religious fugitives from the established church. Goodykoontz paints their economic-religious background by depicting these Scotch-Irish as "poor to begin with, and . . . not accustomed to paying their ministers directly. Many ministers were forced to do secular work, mainly teaching or farming. (Their) congregations sometimes were neglected."[5]

These people were plainly prejudiced on the subject of a professional ministry. After arriving here, Alexander Campbell remained quiet upon this subject for ten or twelve years and then (though I would not mean in the least to impugn his motives) decided to play to the "Frontier American

Gallery" in these matters of support and education of the
ministry. The frontier mind felt, of course, that *anyone*
could do it. *Anyone* could be a minister. In fact, anyone
could "be" almost anything he wanted to be with little or
no preparation. Medicine suffered from this. Teaching, law
and all the learned professions were not exempted. How
could you possibly persuade a frontiersman who had ad-
ministered to every physical need of his family, from delivering a baby to performing minor surgery, that anyone
needed much study to be a doctor? All he needed was experience. All this baggage of European education and professional status had to be "dumped." This was the sort of
thinking that Campbell confronted. It sometimes repelled
him but he had to face it.

I am quite certain that in the silent years both he and his
father experienced some struggle in reconciling themselves
to speak to this common American mind. Their Lockian
Common Sense philosophy prepared them. And under God,
they knew they must do it, but they did not wish to compromise *all* intellectual standards. That much is apparent.
But some compromises came and were made in order to
provide a "tent-making" ministry for the burgeoning frontier. These proved to be the very ones from which this
movement was to suffer longest.

In spite of later attempts (particularly in the establishment of Bethany College), Campbell could not recall, or
reinterpret, his "winged words" of *The Christian Baptist*
regarding the ministry. The frontiersmen heard him the
first time, as they wanted to hear him. Even the publication
of *The Christian System*, aimed at office and order in the
church, did not fully accomplish the expunging of the anti-
clerical record. Nevertheless, this is precisely what Mr.
Campbell and his associates tried to do from 1830 on.

As W. E. Garrison observed:

Long before the first generation of our fathers had passed
from the scene, Disciples of Christ had come to realize that,

though any Christian might properly preach who *could* preach, there was need for a trained ministry and those who intended to devote their lives to this work should be ordained to the ministry.[6]

Every advance is accompanied by some evil but what marks it as an advance is the good outweighs the evil. Such has been the case here. There is no question that Disciples have developed many outstanding laymen because of this situation and its professional ministry has been more sensitive to the common man than most.

Let us look further at the backgrounds of the religious revolution of the nineteenth century and just how concepts of the ministry developed.

First, there are the personal experiences of the principals: the "happenstances," the turn of events, the little dates with destiny. One cannot help wondering if both Campbell and Stone's attitudes toward the ministry might have been different had their experiences varied only slightly. For example, suppose Stone had been associated with a more temperate group of preachers. Or suppose that the turn of events that took Campbell back to Scotland after the shipwreck had brought him to a different sort than the austere John Mitchell (The Seceder Presbyterian). What would have been our history had Mitchell been just a bit more cordial? (Or was it that his house was not as commodious and as suitable to entertaining a guest as those of the Sandemanians, George Fulton and Greville Ewing?) At any rate, the fact that young Alexander Campbell did stay with Fulton and Ewing makes a world of difference. The order of ministry he writes twenty years later could have come from the pen of their mentor, John Glas.

Some ideas on ministerial support should be credited to personal circumstances. One would think by reading most Campbell biographies that he got married in order to have a first child and settle the question of infant baptism. They deal only slightly with his financial independence coming from his marriage to Margaret Brown. And though he is reputed to be the richest man in West Virginia at the time of his death, it is difficult to find anything written concerning the financial rewards that came from the operation of the gristmill and the sawmill upon the Buffalo, to say nothing about the production of the land itself. Campbell's economic position in the community was substantially acquired through the generosity of his father-in-law Brown. One cannot help wondering how history might have been changed if Campbell and the whole Brush Run Church had moved to Zanesville, Ohio in 1814 as they talked and planned of doing but which was prevented by Brown's business proposition which Campbell accepted.

Many a Disciple minister, from then on, has secretly hoped that he, too, might have a "tent-making" ministry similar to Campbell's. This wealth freed him to do all the writing, publishing, studying and the like so important to the Movement. It providentially became his inheritance. But it certainly should not be forgotten that this situation affected his teachings and attitudes in regard to the ministry.

"One of the most persistent patterns in American religious history has been the Americanization of religious expression in this country,"[7] says D. E. Harrell in his fine book, *Quest for a Christian America*. In Disciple concepts of the ministry this has been a recognizable fact. We have been a product, at least in part, of the social and cultural conditions that stand away from, and often against, some New Testament concepts. For example, Campbell's Americanized capitalism put him and Sidney Rigdon at odds.

Rigdon, an early member of the movement, believed that the early church "held all things in common" and he had some Scripture to prove it. The showdown occurred between the two in 1830 when Rigdon left, beaten in an argument with Campbell, to become a convert to Mormonism, perhaps its most important convert. In that sect he found more fertile soil for *his* particular first century doctrines.

What emerged in the first fifty years of the Campbell-Stone Movement was a concept of ministry found in an essay of the early eighteen-thirties entitled, "The Christian Ministry," which Campbell later included in *The Christian System,* in 1839. It was largely produced in the 1835 "Extra" of *The Millennial Harbinger.* There is good reason to believe that this formulation on the ministry was made by Campbell after considerable discussion with his father and Robert Richardson.

Campbell begins this formulation by observing that "for the setting up of the Christian Institution officers extraordinary were needed." Miraculous powers were given by Our Lord to Apostles and Prophets in the first century, but both these offices and the extraordinary gifts have ceased. The church now requires only an "ordinary ministry." So Campbell said:

> The standing and immutable ministry of the (present) Christian community is composed of Bishops, Deacons, and Evangelists. Of each of these there is but one order, though possessing great diversities of gifts, there have been bishops, deacons, and evangelists, with both ordinary and extraordinary gifts. Still the office is now, and ever was, the same.[8]

In addition to being ordinary, i.e., wherever the church was to be found, these three offices were regarded as being perpetual because of the continuing need of the church. As to their functions, Campbell wrote:

> *Bishops,* whose office it is to preside over, to instruct and to edify the community—to feed the church of the Lord with knowledge and understanding—and to watch for their souls as those that must give account to the Lord at his appearing and his kingdom, compose the first class. *Deacons,* or servants—whether called treasurers, almoners, stewards, doorkeepers, or messengers—constitute the second. . . . *Evangelists,* however, though a class of public functionaries created by the church, do not serve it directly;

but are by it sent out into the world, and constitute the third class of functionaries belonging to the Christian system.[9]

He added that laymen could do everything that ministers could. Indeed, they had the right to "preach, baptize, and dispense the supper, as well as to pray for all men, when circumstances demand it."[10]

However, according to Campbell, this did *not* dispense with the need for order and office in the church. He warned against thinking that *any* unqualified person had the right to assume the responsibilities, imposed by this immutable ministry. While one may doubt that before 1835 he would have insisted on an ordained ministry, he felt now that persons entrusted with the ordinary ministries of the church should be "set-apart" by the imposition of hands, prayer and fasting. Moreover, he felt that the Christian society which was built in accord with the fundamental Christian principles laid down by the apostles "has the only true, real apostolic succession of divine authenticity, and therefore we as a Christian community, have it."[11] So, these were offices of ministry generally accepted by Disciples in the first part of the nineteenth century. Of course, they presumed some variant interpretation of New Testament teachings. The problem posed by the knowledge that one man held all three offices in the New Testament was never satisfactorily resolved. Moreover, the basic equalitarian views of the constituency almost always prevailed. A former teacher of mine use to say, "when the New Testament was in conflict with Jacksonian Democracy, as far as many early American Disciples were concerned, the New Testament always lost."[12]

The real significance of this well-developed pronouncement on order and office of the ministry in *The Millennial Harbinger* of 1835 is that it represents a considerable reversal of Campbell's previous position in regard to support of the ministry. In a dozen years from 1820, he had come from the anti-clericalism of *The Christian Baptist,* with its clear inference that anyone who accepted pay for preaching was a part of the damnable "Kingdom of the Clergy," a "hireling priest" and all that, to an ordered and ordained ministry that could enter into "social contract" with congregations.

Having taken this position, he continued to develop it through his life. He saw Elders, Presbyters and Bishops as the same, though he preferred the latter title. To the consternation of many readers of today he refers to his Baptist friends as "Bishop Semple" or "Bishop Vardeman."[13] He encouraged the local people in Bethany to use this title for the Elders of the church, but according to inside information upon this matter, and in spite of the pronouncements in the favor of plurality of such, no one was called "Bishop" at Bethany but Campbell himself.[14]

What were the reasons for the change in these dozen years? Perhaps we will never know, but here are at least five possibilities.

1. The basic objection to a "status ministry" was more clearly defined in Campbell's mind. His objection shifted in accent from the *authority* of the "clergy," their "fixed salaries" and "splendid meeting houses," to the *abuses* of the same. This is a natural development in reasoning with a mature mind. While preacher pay was approved as early as 1831, Campbell was "careful to add that no recognition of the clergy as 'spiritual fathers' was to go with the pay."[15]

2. It had become necessary to provide support for such evangelists as Walter Scott, who did not have the accumulated resources of an Alexander Campbell.

3. The need to devote more time to the preaching of the gospel was greater than first envisioned in 1820. This country was simply growing more rapidly than Campbell had anticipated.

4. His growing dissatisfaction with the unlearned, uneducated and uncouth Baptist preachers. This I think, is the "hidden agenda" behind the dissolution of the Mahoning Association and obviously a factor in the Redstone Association.

5. The joining with the Stoneites, who, though they, too, had been anti-clerical, had not been as outspoken as Campbell. Mr. Campbell could not have been completely unaware that the potential increase in the Movement was greater from these Kentuckians and Carolinians than from the Western Reserve. He did not seek to enlarge differences with them. Garrison and DeGroot are right when they say, concerning Stone and his associates, that they:

> . . . . . . perhaps remembering their orderly Presbyterian background even while repudiating the authority of presbyteries and synods, had at least the beginnings of a method of obtaining a responsible ministry. Reports from the churches carefully distinguished between "Elders" (meaning ordained ministers) and "unordained preachers." Stone criticized those who thought that a church could "induct into the ministerial office"; He considered that function as belonging to the "bishops and elders." If a minister is charged with "preaching doctrine contrary to the Gospel" he should be examined by a "conference of bishops and elders." The idea was that the ministry as a whole, or by conference groups, should have power to protect the churches from erratic or unworthy ministers.[16]

Such control, however, was never completely exercised. But from 1835 on, the need for it was expressed again and again both by the "Christians" and the "Disciples."

In the eighteen-twenties, Campbell became a leading figure in a completely American struggle against "status theocrats," who generally were the educated, Eastern clergy, predominantly Presbyterian, Episcopal and Congregational. These were determined to impress their religious, educational and moral values upon this young nation. Among their chief tools were the Bible and Missionary Societies. Thus, such organizations became the target of *The Christian Baptist*. When the Eastern group became aware of Campbell and the others with him on the frontier, they most generally expressed dismay at the lack of education of the ministers of the entourage. This Campbell never denied. Fortunately for us, he also resisted the temptation to "spiritualize" the matter. As quickly as possible, he led in efforts to establish educational enterprises, though one is tempted to think that he felt that Bethany would be sufficient. The curricula of these early colleges probably reveals a reaction to the Eastern "theocrats." At first there was to be little Bible teaching offered, and, of course, no courses in theology, not even from a historical survey point of view. This emphasis upon a liberal education was not an unmixed benefit for our people, but it very quickly left us with a ministry that picked up its theological education here and there. This was an important facet of the Campbell-Stone Revolution.

There is a striking similarity in the development at about the same time of the Cumberland Presbyterians. The Cumberland schism in the Presbyterian Church was brought about largely by the lack of elasticity in the church, particularly in regard to the frontier ministry. The Presbyterian Church simply refused to accept lower standards for ministers there and the Cumberland group broke away.[17] Similarly, the argument that James O'Kelly first had with Asbury had primarily to do with the proposition that "a preacher be given the right to appeal to the conference if he didn't like his appointment."[18] Of course he lost this struggle and he left.

For Disciples this fussing and fuming had also to do with very practical matters, such as whether or not a congregation was going to have a minister at all, or how he was to be supported. It had to do with the proposition of whether or not communities were to go without the Lord's Supper for months until some Elder would get around to administering it. Clearly, Campbell and Stone were practical men who looked for workable solutions having some support in Scripture. Concepts and practices of the ministry that had their relevancy to another time for another society in another land were simply abandoned in the face of this pragmatism.

Throughout 1836, acting in his responsibility as associate editor of *The Millennial Harbinger,* Robert Richardson made many practical applications of the general principles of the previous years' Extra on the ministry, which reveals his connection with the development of ideas in *The Christian System.* Among other things he advised new frontier congregations that contributions for "light and fuel" and "to provide a meeting place" were *not* "to the Lord" but had to do entirely with the "social comfort" of the church members.[19] He described the real offerings as the funds given on the Lord's day *for His* service in relieving the poor and for the proclamation of the gospel.

His final article contains instructions upon how a church is to proceed when there is no one qualified or "desirous" of performing the work of elder, deacon, or evangelist.[20] His proposal of division of labor would do the proponents of a functional order of church life good. For even in such circumstances he warned of one or two members doing everything. He seems almost willing to settle for a church without a full-time ministry; but it becomes increasingly evident by the time that the next two decades have passed that the only possible answer was in some other course. Finally, ministers simply had to be found regardless of their qualifications. Said Campbell:

> We want a few learned men; but we want a thousand well
> read Bible men, who have read and studied and can repeat

the names of all of the books in the Old and New Testaments, and say something about the authors, dates, occasions and designs of each and everyone of them; who have read the history of the Hebrew, Greek, Roman and Protestant Churches; and who can speak the English language according to Murray's Grammer.[21]

If such a supply of men could be found, if enough could become Bishops and Evangelists and support themselves otherwise, later, said Campbell, would come that "efficient institution . . . over which is Christ . . . with its Bishops and Deacons at home and its Evangelists abroad, wholly devoted to the faithful discharge of their respective trusts."[22] For many this meant a "tent-making" ministry for the time being if they were to share in the Reformation. Most farmed and preached. Others were teachers, blacksmiths, and frontier businessmen.

Many were not ordained. If a local Bishop spoke convincingly and with knowledge of the Scripture, he often gained a reputation as a preacher and began his work among the churches. As far as credentials were concerned, when any were to be had, these came from their local churches. Indeed, sometimes when attempting to check these credentials, the "sending" congregation was found to be nonexistent, usually having dropped out from another westward migration.

More should be said concerning the wives and families of these ministers. It was really they, who made these "tent-making" ministries possible. They stayed home, tended the farm, cared for the livestock, planted and harvested the crops so that the father of the household could go abroad preaching. The attempt to have local elders continue to care for the growing congregations was by 1840 largely failing. Elijah Goodwin reported in 1849 that, after an extensive visit among the churches in Indiana:

In various parts I find small congregations that have been formed by transient evangelists and that are now left without any regular preaching or teaching. They have not talent enough among them to make their meetings interesting or instructive, and therefore, they are poorly attended. They are not able to sustain competent evangelists, and hence, if something is not done and done speedily they must soon cease to exist.[23]

In 1842, Campbell himself agrees, as he writes:

The cause of reformation would ere now have overrun the whole community, but for two causes: *One*—untaught new converts. *Second*—is a class of unsent, unaccomplished, uneducated advocates who plead it; amongst whom, too, have been found a number of persons of immoral character.[24]

He complained further that the movement had lost ground in finding an adequate ministry because:

Another portion of our more gifted and ingenuous cohorts have addicted themselves to the unenviable task of public censors of the senior theologians. Boys in their teens, or youths . . . are now gravely and learnedly exposing the errors of Luther, Calvin, Wesley, the descendants of Dort, Westminster, Trent . . . and others . . . with as much self approbation and secret relish as the most exquisite sensualist devours a favorite dish.[25]

These general practices upon the part of unqualified persons, Campbell says, adds to the "profanation of the evangelical office." These were men who chiefly sought to be known for their pugnaciousness, seeking popularity through debate and other activities of this sort, which would enable them to draw crowds without any substantial credentials and to abandon them without any pastoral responsibility.

The ink had scarcely dried on *The Christian System* before Campbell and Stone were pleading for needed cooperation to save and make responsible more ministers. Says Campbell, "We want cooperation. Some brethren are afraid of its power; others complain of its inefficiency." Campbell then recalls for his readers' benefit that Stone had written him in 1838 regarding the alarming loss of

ministers to "worldly positions to make enough to live on."
Says Campbell, "The venerable elder (Stone) is most dis-
consolate and broken-hearted at the scenes which are beginning to appear about him." Elucidating on this, Campbell says that where there is no cooperation in the support
of the ministry, tragedies are occurring in the lives and
families of the most devoted. While dedicated evangelists
are needed indeed, he says, "we also want the same sort
of citizens in all the churches who employ them and who
send them forth."[26]

As a matter of fact, the "tent-making" ministry did *not*
solve the support problem for the church *or* its ministers.
Not being able to devote sufficient time to their farms
and fields, preachers often failed in business and in their
occupational tasks. All through the years, down to this very
day, the ministerial relief rolls have been composed largely
of men, or their widows, who "supported themselves" in
order to preach the gospel.

The fact is they have largely encouraged the church in
the practice of poor stewardship. Lack of commitment always leads to weakness. This weakness, which through the
years has threatened the life of this communion and has
been its number one enemy, has been this type of "tent-
making" stewardship. It has often simply been an attempt
to find a cheap way! But coupled with the loss in stewardship, has been the wasting of its leadership. We have lost
from preaching, teaching, and pastoral ministry, hosts of
men and women throughout the years. They have truly
been servants without hire.

True, we can rationalize by saying that some of them
have become good laymen. Others have taken up service
with other communions. And while I am grateful for this,
others would say "they were lost to the denominations."
This didn't start just yesterday, or with any "dying brotherhood" that some convention speaker memorialized. Most of

these simply "fade away" into other vocations. For Disciples, since 1960, our studies reveal that almost 900 have been lost. In this we counted only those who had either attained a listing as a resident pastor or staff member in a church or who were classified as a middler in seminary or above.[27]

My point is that this problem of unemployed ministers and unfilled pulpits began at the very dawn of our brotherhood. Later on, we will see that the pastorate was such an expensive experience for the preaching elder-evangelist that it was threatening. So, for many in the nineteenth century it was safer to stay with teaching, or farming, as far as personal finances were concerned. In some ways, working as a traveling evangelist or editing a paper offered more security. Almost, as it began, the "tent-making" ministry was crashing on economic rocks.

If that didn't sink it, it went aground in the shallows of moral perfidy. In 1841, "Raccoon" John Smith wrote Campbell regarding the dangers of endorsing preachers by "editors" (in this case he meant Campbell's endorsement). Some common names, like his own, made for possible confusion. Campbell had evidently endorsed a John McVay, because he thought him to be another more reliable man by this same name. Smith then describes this imposter, whom Campbell had unwittingly approved, as a cheating horsetrader, who abandoned a blind wife, and later fathered an illegitimate child. Smith wryly remarked, "seven or eight years ago (he) fell into the current reformation, but no reformation from his wicked conduct."[28]

These sorts of cases, far too abundant across the American frontier, caused both Campbell and Stone to reconsider the possibility of some Presbyterial authority within the church. Campbell wrote:

> The Christian Ministry are responsible to the Lord and his people for faithful discharge of their duties as the presiding rulers of the church, and as having the ministry of the Word

committed to their hands for those districts of the country in which the Lord has placed them.[29]

He then goes on to use Kentucky as an example and to suggest that the ministers of Kentucky should bind themselves together in some form, in order to protect the church. Campbell was beginning to see that an irresponsible ministry was as bad or worse than a status ministry.

I certainly would not want to leave the impression that *all* who ministered in this way were unworthy. Most were quite sacrificial. The sacrifices of their families, as I have indicated, were monumental. They did like the wide open spaces, as a rule. D. E. Harrell observes that most of our fathers were opposed to cities and were in favor of an economic individualism largely based on "Jeffersonian Agrarianism."[30] They were a genuine part of the frontier American Society which was individualistic and optimistic. As they saw it, the revolution was being won. Every man was a king. The individualism, independency and the right of every man and every congregation to do as it pleased was not to be abrogated.

There were to be no "reverends" in this new society, even if there were bishops. One needed to be careful even there that he spelled that word with a small "b" unless he used it just before someone's name. To be a "servant not for hire," or the opposite of the "hireling clergy," was to owe no man anything, expecially when it came to authority, even if you might owe him money or a few bushels of corn. The independency toward the ministry which Campbell had spawned in *Christian Baptist* days, had found ready acceptance in the cultural situation of western America. He often found himself explaining his position regarding it. In the Purcell debate, he declared:

> I am sorry that he (Purcell) seemed to take advantage of my acknowledging myself as a friend to Bishops and Deacons in the church . . . Let no one imagine, however, that I am at all opposed to order and government in the church. As

far as concerns oversight, or the having of Bishops to preside over the flock, I am Episcopalian. I am for having
Presbyters or elders in every church. I do not believe in a
church without Presbyters or Bishops. So far, I am both a
Presbyterian and an Episcopalian.[31]

In one form or another, this sort of statement was made
many times, but the crisis in the ministry of the movement
continued to grow. It seems to me that it came to a climax
in 1849.

Many folk have an interesting concept of that first annual
convention held in Cincinnati that year. It is based more
on subsequent controversy and hearsay than fact. They will
tell you that it was held primarily to organize a missionary
society. As a matter of fact, this was only one of several
items upon the agenda. And, in the announcements, this
item was listed primarily as a proposed "committee" of the
existing Bible Society. An item of considerably greater concern which occupied much of the last half of the convention
had to do with the ministry. And for it, there seems to me
to have been much prior consideration.

Concern for the condition of the ministry had risen stead-
ily since 1835. Discussion was not entirely doctrinal, for it
arose often around the matter of support. For example,
Campbell, writing in *The Millennial Harbinger* in 1840
under the topic, "The Duty and Means of Supporting
Evangelists," says:

> In the first place, then, one *"who labors in the word and
> teaching,"* whether he be a *teaching elder* located in a
> special charge, or an *evangelist* sent abroad, ought to give
> himself wholly to this work—he ought to "preach the word,"
> and "to be instant in season and out of season" as ordained
> by the Apostle.[32]

He concludes,

> The Lord ordained that those who waited on the altar
> should live on the offerings presented on that altar. Even
> so has the Lord now ordained that they who preach the

Gospel should live by their calling and find their temporal, spiritual and eternal interests all promoted by faithfully serving the Lord in the Gospel of his son.[33]

While the above citation does not include a reference to First Corinthians, Nine from which it is obviously paraphrased, Campbell sums up the problem, by stating that:

Men have called themselves faithful laborers for the Lord while all the week laboring for themselves as well as on the Sabbath—six days under pay on the farm or in school, and on the seventh in the pulpit. This has often occurred.[34]

And this, he said, is an abuse of the Lord's ordinance.

If, as some think, Walter Scott came to the 1849 Convention as a specially instructed delegate from Campbell, it is obvious that this instruction was primarily to deal with the matter of the ministry. In a forthright speech before the convention, Scott said:

I never feel so much like being angry, as when I am compelled to sit in the sacred stand with men of doubtful character. I feel degraded by the contact.[35]

All of this was addressed to the so-called "third resolution," which was before the convention and which had to do with guarding congregations against unworthy preachers.

Just before the convention, Campbell, writing specifically regarding his experiences in the Redstone Association, with considerable implication to ministers, some of whom doubtless remained around the campfires of the reformation movement to that very hour said:

I had unfortunately formed a very unfavorable opinion of the Baptist preachers as then introduced to my acquaintance, as narrow, contracted, illiberal and uneducated men. This, indeed, I am sorry to say, is still my opinion of this ministry of that Association at that day; and whether they are yet much improved, I am without satisfactory evidence.[36]

Who could have known any better than Walter Scott how Campbell felt about the ministry and what ought to be done

at the Cincinnati Convention? Charles L. Loos, an attendant at the convention, said that "the subject had been a
matter of much discussion in our journals and there was a
general feeling in the main that something should be done
to put a stop to this grievous offense amongst us."[37] Indiana
delegates had come to the convention instructed to "secure
the churches against imposters and traveling vagrants."[38]

A general committee had been appointed, of which Walter Scott was the head, to prepare the agenda for the convention. This included a statement on the ministry. Campbell was not at the convention because of illness. Much
speculation has been made in regard to the real cause of
his absence. When one reads the proceedings of the convention and observes the activities of Walter Scott, W. K.
Pendleton and others close to Campbell in behalf of Presbyterial controls, it would seem altogether possible that
Campbell felt that such a knotty problem could best be
handled in his absence. Had he been there, debate would
have been considerably throttled because his views certainly prevailed whenever made known. Scott seemed prepared on the subject of the ministry. He called for considerable regulation. It seems in accord with what Campbell
had just been requesting in *The Millennial Harbinger.*

In its original form, this so-called "third resolution" was
a simple statement that the convention recommend to the
churches, not to countenance as a preacher, "any man who
is not sustained and acknowledged by two or more
churches." But in true Disciple fashion some felt that this
went too far, and others, not far enough. The result was
that the resolution was sent to a select committee, composed of Walter Scott, D. S. Burnet, John Young, Samuel
Ayres, H. D. Palmer, J. T. Johnson, Carroll Kendrick,
W. K. Pendleton, J. T. Barclay, and John O'Kane. It was
reworded. It came out of the committee even stronger in its
presbyterial tone.

Carroll Kendrick, then of Harrodsburg, Kentucky, later

of Texas and California seems to have been the only member of the committee to object to the threat to congregational authority.[39]He took the debate to the floor and was joined by others in the assembly who expressed themselves "fearful that in attempting to remedy evils, we might produce greater evils," so the Friday afternoon meeting was adjourned without a decision.

When the evening session opened for discussion, it was limited to slightly more than one hour. George Campbell of Indiana made a plea that a strong position be taken on this matter as the delegates from the state meeting of Indiana had previously requested. After a very abbreviated debate (apparently a compromise had been reached) and with the feeling the following might not be so offensive to the churches, this resolution unanimously passed:

> WHEREAS, it appears that the cause of Christianity has suffered from the imposition of false brethren upon the churches, therefore,
>
> RESOLVED that we recommend to the churches the importance of great care and rigid examination before they ordain men to the office of the evangelist. And
>
> RESOLVED that this convention earnestly recommend to the congregations to countenance no evangelist who is not well reported for piety and proper evangelical qualifications, and that they be rigid and critical in their examination of such reports.[35]

Allen R. Moore summarizes Campbell's attitude concerning the convention, by saying:

> Mr. Campbell did not admit that he wished a sort of ministerial presidency (of the convention), yet he insisted that there must be some general organization which the elders or ministers must furnish.[40]

This would lead us to agree with W. E. Garrison that at the first brotherhood-wide convention primary consideration was given "the problem of obtaining an orderly and meaningful content in the ordination of ministers, and lifting (the ministry) above a purely local significance."[41]

Both the church and its ministers wanted to be free. However, in many ways it was beginning to be seen that this freedom could become an abuse. Traveling evangelists could be irresponsible. Unworthy ministers could take advantage of churches. Moreover, congregations could take advantage of ministers and this brought its tragic end in lack of support and its related problems for the most committed men. No less a conservative than Moses E. Lard mournfully wrote of this situation regarding the ministry. He said:

> The reformation for which we plead is the grandest achievement of the century in which we live. Our wonder is that in so short a time it should ever have reached the degree of perfection it has obviously attained. That in its origin no errors should have been committed is something none had reason to expect. We are thankful these errors were few; and still more thankful that we lived to see them at least partially corrected. Among the errors with which we set out was that of inveighing against the "hireling system" as we were pleased to phrase it. This was unfortunate, and today we are still reaping the bitter fruits of it.[42]

So the ministry of the Campbell-Stone Movement had been set free. Free from the authoritarianism of Europe, free from artificial and ecclesiastical distinctions between ministers and laymen, free from being hireling priests of sectarianism or proud graduates of theological seminaries, free from written creeds and precise formulations of faith. Yet the minister was bound by many limitations, often self-imposed, bound by lack of support and stewardship of the pioneer congregations, but *most of all*, he was a *free minister in a free society*.

As an evangelist, or preaching elder, in the Campbell-Stone Movement at the middle of the nineteenth century, he knew two things basic to this new freedom: *First*, he must be a servant. He was indeed a servant of the servants. *Secondly,* he knew there was no human rank above his in the church. For him, this was sufficient assurance of freedom.

He needed to discover that as a minister, or servant, this did not mean that there was no discipline—that there is no true freedom without responsibility. The best of our early preachers soon discovered this, and from them we could learn that lesson again. For them, this included *first,* the discipline of our Lord, as well as self-discipline, plus that taught by the example of others and motivated by love for one another.

Campbell's favorite term for this movement was "the reformation." Much later there were those who called it, "the restoration." I have referred to it as "a revolution," for such it was for those in the public ministry. They were not only in a revolt against something, but they were experiencing an "emergence," a "change," or a "turn," which is a more accurate and positive definition of the term "revolution." They not only came from a historical place into this culture, as we have said, they were going some place, confident of victory.

All sorts of men responded to this call. Some were aware of the fact that society itself was in revolution at that time and that religion was in the midst of radical change. Many came from the denominations and were almost immediately set at the task of evangelizing. There was scanty preparation for others, as they turned from the plow and workman's bench to the pulpit. There was revolt within the revolution. Education was sought as a solution. Organization was proposed as an answer. There was a constant appeal to self-discipline, congregational discipline, discipline under the Book and under our Lord. But above all, there was individualism, committed individualism for the most part. Lack of support made them more "ragged" than "rugged." Scores of men "left all" and followed; many of whom could not be recalled today, but upon whose names the eyes of a student must reverently fall as he goes through the old issues of magazines and papers. Their bones lie in humble graves beside the trails that ran west. For the most part, they had a valid, workable concept of their ministry.

It is easy to sentimentalize about them and I know that that is the last thing that they would wish. If it were possible, I would like to acquaint you with some of them as we move along. They were certainly *not* "a hireling clergy," but they were often "servants without hire."

NOTES

1. Samuel Stennett, "On Jordan's Stormy Banks" *The King's Praise*—A General Purpose Songbook (Cincinnati: Standard Publishing Co., 1927), p. 172.
2. Richard Baxter, *The Reformed Pastor,* ed. Hugh Martin (London: S.C.M. Press Ltd., 1956), p. 9.
3. John Smith, *Lectures on the Nature and End of the Sacred Office and on the Dignity, Duty, Qualifications and Character of the Sacred Order* (Baltimore: A. Neal, Publisher, 1812).
4. B. W. Stone, Quoted by Earl I. West in Vol. I, *The Search For the Ancient Order* (Nashville: Gospel Advocate Co., 1949), pp. 18-19.
5. Harry G. Goodykoontz, *The Minister in the Reformed Tradition* (Richmond, Virginia: John Knox Press, 1963), pp. 85-86.
6. W. E. Garrison, *Heritage and Destiny: An American Religious Movement Looks Ahead* (St. Louis: The Bethany Press, 1961), p. 73.
7. David Edwin Harrell, *Quest For A Christian America* (Nashville, Tennessee: Disciples of Christ Historical Society, 1966), p. 12.
8. Alexander Campbell, *The Christian System* (St. Louis: Christian Publishing Co., 1890), p. 83.
9. *Ibid.,* p. 84.
10. *Ibid.,* p. 87.
11. *Debate Between Rev. A. Campbell and Rev. N. L. Rice on . . . Christian Baptism* (Lexington, Kentucky, 1844), p. 583.
12. Dean E. Walker, class notes, Butler University School of Religion, 1941-42.
13. W. E. Garrison and A. T. DeGroot, *The Disciples of Christ—A History* (St. Louis: Christian Board of Publication, 1948), p. 177.
14. Dwight Stephenson, "Ordained Elders: A Brief Historical Review" *The Scroll,* Vol. LVIII (Autumn, 1966), p. 20.
15. O. R. Whitley, *The Trumpet Call of Reformation* (St. Louis: Bethany Press, 1959), p. 89.
16. W. E. Garrison and A. T. DeGroot, *The Disciples of Christ—A History,* p. 210.
17. H. G. Goodykoontz, *The Minister in the Reformed Tradition,* p. 92.

18. Earl I. West, *The Search for the Ancient Order* (Nashville: Gospel Advocate Co., 1949), Vol. I, p. 9.
19. Robert Richardson, Replies to F. W. Emmons, as well as "Order 1, 2 and 3" *The Millennial Harbinger,* Vol. VII (July, Sept. and Oct., 1836), pp. 326, 424, 519.
20. *Ibid.,* p. 425.
21. A. Campbell, Editorial, *The Millennial Harbinger,* Vol. II (June, 1838), p. 270.
22. A. Campbell, *The Christian System,* p. 90.
23. *The Christian Record,* 1849, quoted by C. W. Cauble, *Disciples of Christ in Indiana* (Indianapolis: Meigs Publishing Co., 1930), p. 100.
24. Alexander Campbell, editorial, *The Millennial Harbinger,* Vol. VI (June, 1842), p. 242.
25. *Ibid.,* p. 245.
26. Alexander Campbell, Correspondence with B. W. Stone, *The Millennial Harbinger,* Vol. II (June, 1838), pp. 267-271.
27. My own studies on drop outs begun in 1960 from College, Seminary, Disciple Yearbook and Pension Fund records.
28. John Smith, Letter, *The Millennial Harbinger,* Vol. V (November, 1841), p. 536.
29. Alexander Campbell, *The Millennial Harbinger,* Vol. VI (August, 1842), p. 329.
30. David Edwin Harrell, *Quest for a Christian America,* pp. 62-68.
31. Alexander Campbell, *A Debate on the Roman Catholic Religion* (Cincinnati: Rowe Publishers, 1837), pp. 36-37.
32. Alexander Campbell, "The Duty and Means of Supporting Evangelists-No. 1," *The Millennial Harbinger,* Vol. IV (April, 1840), p. 181.
33. *Ibid.,* p. 182.
34. Alexander Campbell, *The Millennial Harbinger,* Vol. IV (January, 1840), p. 48.
35. Walter Scott, Quoted by Chas. Louis Loos, *"Our First General Convention"* (Louisville: Guide Publ. Co., 1891), p. 44.
36. Alexander Campbell, "Anecdotes, Incidents and Facts," *The Millennial Harbinger,* Vol. V (June, 1848), p. 38.
37. Chas. Louis Loos, *Our First General Convention,* p. 44.
38. *Report of the Proceedings of the General Convention of the Christian Churches of the United States of America held in Cincinnati, October 23-25, 1849* (Cincinnati: American Depository, 1849), p. 11, p. 32.
39. *Ibid.,* p. 35.
40. Allen R. Moore, *Alexander Campbell and the General Convention* (St. Louis: Christian Board of Publication, 1914), p. 38.
41. W. E. Garrison and A. T. DeGroot, *The Disciples of Christ—A History,* p. 246.
42. Moses E. Lard, "The Support of Aged Preachers," *Lard's Quarterly,* Vol. 2 (October, 1866), p. 380.

II

Pastors - Evangelists - Bishops
AND SOMETIMES
Deacons

It was not a mere attempt at levity that I suggested the possibility of a "sometimes deacon." This venerable office of ministry, named by Campbell as one of the "immutable three," has often been the brunt of jokes. In reality, it is a most purely liturgical office, if that word with its Greek meaning, "*work*" is taken literally.

The Greek word, *diakonos,* is derived from the verb, "to serve" or "to minister." So, our word, "minister," is the simple Latin translation. It is the most frequently used word in the New Testament for minister, or ministry. Disciples use it more often than any other. It is the all inclusive word, covering the "varieties of service" listed in First Corinthians, Twelve. There are scores of other references. Perhaps the one written latest was to Timothy when he was admonished to be a "good minister (diakonos) of Christ Jesus." (1 Tim. 4: 6)

Campbell built the order outlined in *The Christian System* with one eye on Ephesians, Four and another on the contemporary scene. Thus, with both this Scripture and the need at hand, he emphasized the role of the evangelist and presbyter-bishop. This prevailed and left the deacon as more or less a local functionary, who is caricaturized today in "Church Chuckles."

One hundred years ago in Indianapolis, there lived a man named Butler Kennedy Smith. It was not his original intention to be a preacher. He had a thriving blacksmith business located near the National Road. To translate it to a modern picture, it would be like being the leading Chevrolet dealer today. He was a prominent citizen, one of the organizers of Central Christian Church and a man of some physical and mental strength. In fact, he had the proportions and weight to have qualified for the Green Bay Packers' line. He describes how he was "roped" into being a deacon. Those first meetings of the first church of the Campbell-Stone Movement in Indiana's capital city were all too typical for the times. They elected two bishops because, of course, they *had to have more than one.* Neither of the elected "felt qualified" and so failed to serve. Several meetings of the little congregation went by outdoing the Quakers in silence, when at last, Smith volunteered to "lead" in worship including the singing, Bible reading and prayer. The Lord's supper was finally celebrated.

This experience led Smith to begin the process of preparing himself and he developed a concern for the church and its ministry rarely matched since. He educated himself, mastering Greek and English to the extent that he wrote two books and many tracts. He aided in the establishment of several churches in central Indiana and was so highly regarded that Campbell himself sought him out in one of his rare visits to the city. Campbell stayed away from Indianapolis because he said the climate and terrain there were detrimental to health, but in 1850 he braved the unfriendly elements when it became apparent that Disciples in Indiana were about to establish in this growing community a competitive college to Bethany.[1]

B. K. Smith's book, *The Scriptural Organization,* is one of the best that we have out of this period on the ministry, and it is worth the time of any reader. He makes two significant points. One arose out of his experience as an elected deacon. He could never quite see how the work of the deacon described in the New Testament Pastorals could be equated with the general interpretation in Campbell's *Christian System.* He wrote:

> Now I appeal to the candor of every intelligent reader of these pages if the foregoing popular view of the subject (of deacon) does not turn into ridicule the grave array of requisite qualifications laid down in Paul's instructions to Timothy which we have been examining? I have heard of such things as loading a cannon to kill a fly, and I have seen men display a large sum of money to pay an insignificant bill, but I cannot believe that the *All-wise Lord* would insist on such profound and matured qualifications, both in deed and heart, in one whose official duty was comprised of serving tables, handling and dispersing money and sweeping, firing and lighting up meeting houses.[2]

His second contribution also cut across accepted ideas. He proposed that each congregation should have *but one* bishop, or overseer. By 1870, Disciple "bishops" were plural in number and usually *not* preachers. The preacher either "traveled in" or remained under an annual "call," and was regarded, and often called, "The Evangelist." Smith argued that the Ephesian Elders of the Book of Acts were not bishops and that the word "bishop" itself, in Greek, indicated an office of which there was only one for each congregation. The bishop in Smith's plan was to be the *ex-officio* "president of all meetings, either of the church or of the eldership." He was to preside in person, or deputize someone to fill in his place. Smith added that such a bishop is no better qualified than other deacons, elders and deaconesses to baptize, dispense the Word, administer the sacraments, or even preside at the meeting, but he should do so because this is his office and the church needs order. He added, the bishop has "no *authority* aside from the moral influence (which) his superior age, piety, experience and wisdom entitle him to."[3]

As a matter of fact, much of the problem of understanding the ministerial offices of the church throughout history, according to John Knox, has arisen because many theologians have been so conditioned with Greek thinking that they did not see that the organizations of the earliest churches in the New Testament were built on Jewish ideas, particularly the Sanhedrin, which offered pattern, function, and terminology for the elders. Knox says the word *Episcopé* (bishop) was introduced simply to aid the gentile Christians in understanding the Hebrew concepts of *Presbyteros.*[4]

B. K. Smith's proposals are examples of the frustration Disciples were feeling shortly after the mid-century mark regarding the ministry. He himself was never ordained, and that was, and is, the case for many Disciple preachers. He was also one of the first to express the accompanying anxiety of our people at the coming urbanization of America and to point out the ineffectiveness of a primarily lay ministry for these new cities. He asked, if a Bishop must be "given to hospitality," and if his brethren do not furnish him the means *and* provide the time, how can he possibly fill that part of his office? In cities, this sort of pastoral care and concern was becoming desperately needed. Others, like D. S. Burnet in Cincinnati, recognized it, too.

Smith asked what was wrong with Disciples when they despaired of cities like Fort Worth, feeling that they must remove their institutions from them when they became communities of more than a thousand or so. With such size they were often regarded as places of wickedness to be avoided at all cost. As a matter of fact, Add-Ran College was not the only one that was rushed to the country to keep it pure. The Campbells gave this as an important reason for the location of Bethany. B. K. Smith may have been low in the ranks of the ministry, only a lay deacon, but he saw some of the changes that were coming and he knew better than many others that to be a minister, one must serve. And to render this service to God, it must be done through people where they are, even in a city. Perhaps Disciples will continue ineffective in the cities until they can get an equipping ministry with this sense of mission.

Regarding bishops, Dwight Stevenson believes that Campbell meant to reserve this term primarily for those who spend their full time in oversight of congregations.[5] But, if this were true, this distinction did not catch on in the brotherhood. On the other hand, the idea that "Elder" and "Bishop" were interchangeable terms did, and by nineteen-hundred many ministers were described with the prefix "Elder," while the non-preaching layman, be he elder or deacon, was often addressed as "Brother so-and-so." However, there was *no* consistency in this. The compiled book, *The Holy Spirit—A Symposium* lists on its fly leaf the writers as *Elder* A. B. Jones, *Elder* G. W. Longan, *Elder* T. Munnell, *Elder* J. Z. Taylor and A. Campbell (with no prefix). In the 1860's, not many called themselves "pastor," but when so, the same was often addressed as either "Evangelist" or "Elder," occasionally "Bishop." The last title became unpopular for both preachers and others largely because of the fact that it stressed the matter of ruling, and most of the "rulers" performed this function so poorly that the title soon fell into disrepute. As most came to view it, however, the "Elder" was a local officer who had three functions, namely, to teach, to rule, and to shepherd.

The general practice was to elect elders and deacons to office and there was usually the admonition to ordain them, but there is some doubt that either of these things were regularly done. J. H. Garrison, among many others, was never ordained. That the custom of ordination was not universally practiced is also confirmed by "side comments" like those of F. D. Kershner when he describes these local church offices and traces their New Testament background. He observed that ordination "should still be observed."[6]

Ordination was often viewed as merely induction into office. Many felt God alone could "lay His hand" on a man.[7] Some even argued that there should be *no* election. J. Carroll Stark held this view, remarking that selection by other elders was more in keeping with the Scriptures and that the practice of pure democracy was dangerous, for, he said:

> in the church, or kingdom of heaven, men do not reach equality at once . . . generally the babes born into the kingdom (now) rush from their baptism to the church to enjoy their first opportunity to vote upon a subject of which they have, as yet, no opportunity to learn anything; and often take the church not only from the Lord Jesus, but from qualified to unqualified hands.[8]

Stark, and some others, continued their argument against the status quo by contending that elders, particularly preaching elders, should be appointed under some sort of a Presbyterial system.[9] Also opposing general elective practices but coming out at the opposite pole was Ben Franklin of Indiana, who, in the eighteen-seventies held the view that local elders and deacons were *divinely* appointed.[10] He used this argument to press his objections to pastors. He argued that such elders (divinely appointed) were overseers and, thus, had the responsibility of oversight of the evangelist's work, as well as their own, and all others in the congregation. He added that this should be for them no "lording it over" one another, but a recognition that they were *all* lords under *one* Lord.

While it is true that elders were generally elected and ordained by one local congregation, they sometimes became preaching evangelists. As evangelists, they were not officers of the local congregation served, and it was difficult for them to distinguish and separate their functions when they shifted roles. Campbell doubtless had recognized this problem and said there needed to be "more scrupulosity" concerning evangelists. As he saw it, evan-

gelists were those persons "devoted to the preaching of
the word, to the making of converts, and the planting of
churches."[11] By 1870, the line between "bishops" and
"evangelists" got to be very thin. A bishop, who was
speaking to a group of Christians, would be said to be
"teaching." If there were any unconverted in the crowd,
he would be "preaching," and hence an evangelist.

One might wish that we had maintained some of the
reformed presbyterial idea that ministers who handle
preaching were so appointed *because* of their teaching
ability. Even the administration of the sacraments was, by
the sixteenth century reformers, regarded as visual teaching. The preaching of the Word was audible teaching.[12]
Ultimately it was seen that if there was to be a ministry
at all for the Campbell-Stone congregations, ministers
needed to be selected because of their ability and preparation to teach and to pastor. And that is exactly where the
conflict arose.

It is a mistake to think that the controversy over the
located pastor did not begin until the 1890's. By then, it
was simply an added excuse for debate and division. Had
not the Civil War occupied much of the attention of our
people in the sixties, it would have secured an earlier
prominence.

As a matter of fact, opposition was already aligned by
1865, Moses E. Lard numbered himself in that opposition.
He wrote that year:

> There is no such function or position in the church as that
> of a pastorate to be filled by a special class of men different
> from the elders. . . . Now, in view of the truth as here
> stated, we cannot but feel alarmed at the disposition on the
> part of many of our churches—a disposition which is clearly
> on the increase, to create a new office in the church, and
> to fill it with a class of men wholly unknown to the Bible.[13]

Shortly thereafter, a pseudonymous reader attempted to
put the editor of the *Christian Standard* on the spot in

1869 by asking, "If our congregation is to have a pastor apart from the Bishops, will someone advise us through the STANDARD as to *The Scriptural Status* of such a functionary so as to save embarrassment all around?"[14]

His question was not dodged, Isaac Errett brought forth a whole series of articles and among other things he said:

> I have had the experience of over a quarter of a century as a preacher, pastor and evangelist; but I have never been right sure in what relation I was regarded by the churches I tried to serve. I have usually regarded myself as a pastor when settled in a congregation; but I have often felt that most of the so called elders looked upon me with suspicion as an Elder rather than a pastor.[15]

Later he added,

> It strikes me that our people are exceedingly *fickle* about their pastors; if it can be said they have *any* fixed ideas of a pastorate. Scarcely do they call one, and he has hardly time to reconnoiter the field, when they desire a change. A year is the general rule, and many, when they begin a year are uncertain whether they will be satisfied enough to justify a continuance through it.[16]

Other brotherhood journals through the period of 1869 to 1890 also have many items on this indicating some disagreement in regard to the matter but also affirming the growing practice of calling an evangelist to stay upon the field as a pastor.

In the summary of his general history published in 1950, Earl West,[17] a historian of the Churches of Christ, attributes to D. S. Burnet the idea of making the preacher a pastor, though he admits that this idea was gaining acceptance before the Civil War, and before Burnet supported it. When hard times came after the war, West observes a decline in the practice because the churches "began to expect all the preaching they could get" *without* paying, and "a selfishness settled upon the churches which put many of the preachers into trouble." . . . And, West adds, "any preacher who under-took to teach the congregation out of its selfishness and to stress their duty to support their labors, immediately ran the risk of severe criticism for preaching for money. Many were silent, therefore, preferring insufficient support to criticism."[18]

As the Church of Christ group began to withdraw over the organ and missionary questions at the close of the century, some looked upon the pastor as another point of departure by the diversionists from the New Testament Christian System. But not many supported them on this point.

Papers that were read before ministerial groups both in New York and Ohio in 1877 indicate the direction the mainstream Disciple thought was taking on the matter of pastors. They held the position that pastors are needed and that the Scriptures allowed for such. They warn that the church does not exist for pastors, but the pastor for the church, and that, though not every elder is a pastor, he who feeds, watches over, and takes care of the flock is a pastor in deed and often needs to be better prepared for the task.

W. W. Hayden,[19] reports in 1877 a discussion arising after one of these papers was read for an Ohio ministers' group. He tells of a young minister who explained a common confusion, saying he had recently accepted a church and yet was not chosen as an elder, or a deacon, by the congregation. "What am I?" he asked the group. Hayden says that his question really went unanswered, "yet one brother ventured a negative suggestion. 'First of all,' said this brother preacher, 'divest yourself of any ideas that you are an evangelist.'" Apparently *such pastors were nowhere really related to the church.* However, the reports indicate the general consensus of these ministerial groups in 1877 was that the pastor should be accepted and regarded as a peer and coordinator with other elders.

Inevitably, conflicts began to arise with the over-seer type of elder and the pastor-evangelist. Editors found it necessary to point out that the preacher was not "a hireling, or a clerk or an employee" but a partner with the church, "which should include both material and spiritual things."[20] The matter of need for support for the proclamation of the gospel struggled for recognition in this tension, as the necessity for pastoral guidance and church administration was becoming more and more apparent.

At the time Thomas Munnell wrote his book, *The Care of All The Churches,* certainly by the 1870's at the latest, it was obvious that churches would have settled pastors. His full title is quite revealing. It was *The Care Of All The Churches (Being a Scriptural Statement of the Character, Qualifications, Ordination and Relative Duties of the Christian Ministry, Evangelists, Bishops and Deacons with Special Directions as to the Practical Details of Successful Ministerial Life, Both in the Spiritual and Business Aspects of the Work).* His observations, based upon more than twenty years of serving as an evangelist sent out by the churches in a state or by the General Convention, could allow him to claim some wide knowledge of the church and its needs. He says, "extreme congregationalism has coldly separated every church to itself, and so prevented any united ministerial effort to have a care for all the churches, as to the business department of church life as well as the spiritual."[21] He points out that the apostles and preachers of the New Testament held major responsibility in this business area. He added:

> For a long time the notion has reigned among many Christian people that the labors of the preacher, whether pastor or evangelist, should be strictly confined to his studio, his pulpit and his social calls—that he has, and should have, *no* responsibility as to church finance, discipline or anything that belongs to the business side of religion. This is a mild sort of heresy, but it has wrought incalculable evil, both to the preachers who have thereby neglected all study of these matters, and to the churches which have always needed such aid and seldom received it.[22]

He observed that this has led to a crop of ministers who "take no interest in anything but their sermons—not in finances, because that is the deacons' work; not in discipline, because that is the elders' business."[23] With it all, there were not enough preachers to go around. E. V. Zollars, early in his career, observed:

> There are whole counties in the State of Ohio where once our cause seemed quite prosperous that are now practically without churches. If churches exist they are either dead or dying. The explanation of this deplorable state of things we believe is found in the fact that our ministry has been utterly insufficient to meet the needs of these churches.[24]

But not all folk believed that pastoral care and located pastors were the answer to the congregation's need. Typically the reactionaries contended:

> That "the pastor," standing alone in his rank is unknown in the church founded by the apostles; that the apostles appointed a plurality of pastors in every congregation; that the words "pastor," "elder" and "bishop" are appellations of the same officer and hence the duties of pastors are identical with the duties of elders and bishops for the very sufficient reason that they are the same persons.[25]

But all that men like David Lipscomb, Tolbert Fanning and Ben Franklin,[26] could offer as an alternative was a "tent-making," "off and on" ministry, with "in and out" itinerant evangelists who were running deeper and deeper into problems. Nevertheless, by the 1890's they brought considerable agitation against the "one man system," as they preferred to call the settled pastor. Both Garrison and Errett, stood together in the *Evangelist* and *Standard* in supporting the pastors and the need for such, by whatever title, to serve the church in growing communities. As W. E. Garrison a generation later pointed out, this argument against pastors found its definite object of attack in a word rather than in a thing." This word was *clerical domination* which was an idea that Campbell had implanted in

Christian Baptist days, and which was feared with a holy horror. They attacked this usurpation of the clergy, but, as Garrison observes, "there was not much clerical usurpation to attack."[27] There just wasn't much to usurp in such a non-authoritative free church. The word "pastor" was attacked only because it seemed to stand against the authority and the plurality of elders.

But those who enjoyed attack for attack's sake more often chose an onslaught on the word, *Reverend*. This title was attached to many pastors, whether they wanted it or not. Some feared it and counted it as a horrible pretention to be carefully guarded against. But it was hung on them, just as the word *doctor* is hung upon physicians. Many men had uninvited experiences concerning this appellation. Others welcomed it because it demonstrated the trivia into which narrow minds can sink. Perhaps the earliest attack on Isaac Errett was that he permitted a "Rev." to appear before his name on a door plate. Explosions immediately followed. Perhaps the best answer given to the problem was that of Thomas Munnell, writing for the *American Christian Review* in 1867. On that occasion, to the embarrassment of the editors, the printer has inadvertently put a "Rev." before a minister's name. It brought forth the usual condemnation of many. Wrote Munnell, without much apology:

> If I had called a minister of the gospel, "Reverend," I had no idea that it would be a sin against the Holy Ghost. Brother Walk states about the truth when he says it simply means that a man is a preacher and is certainly a very brief statement of the fact. The term to me is not a desirable one on account of the abuse of it by others, but in itself it is as harmless as any other.[28]

There was, and is, probably no more nobler or warmer title than "preacher." Why more disciples didn't embrace this term has always puzzled me.

Many felt that this nineteenth century argument over

title and position greatly weakened the movement. Perhaps it did. An editorial in *The Evangelist* in the first issue of 1880 said, "the absurd distinction of clergy and laity is the off-spring of Judaism and Paganism combined." It is then described as an iniquity which encourages a longing for a religious aristocracy which ultimately places the common people of the church under the feet of their spiritual leaders. The result of this, said the writer, is always "a priestly caste system."[29]

Perhaps J. C. Stark was the true radical of his day, since he allowed that women could be elders, an idea unheard of in nineteenth century Christendom. He felt that unrestrained congregationalism was threatening the very existence of the Campbell-Stone Movement and wrote:

> The most fatal error made, among us, as a people, is the idea of the independency of little gatherings of disciples, over whom there is no instructor, or even advisor permitted. They are like little villages organizing themselves with a mayor and town council, and denying the right of country, state or general government to interfere in any way with anything they may do.[30]

He describes the officers and leaders of these "bands," as "babes," who before they are dry, are "ready to vote on the '*calling*' of a preacher, scorning the advice of age, and experience, and study by men full of the Holy Spirit; whose competence has been known for years." Such congregations, he says, "*elect* elders, *call* evangelists, *try* pastors, when they have erred from the truth, or in life, set up a rebellion against the King of all kings, by making their little band independent of the brotherhood of Christ."[31] He adds, "How often some old *pretend* elder, has been *elected* to office, by a system of political chicanery, which would have disgraced a curb-stone politician, to lord it over God's heritage; and he holds on to his place, until the cause of Christ goes down, and the sacrifice of many is thrown away, and souls are sent to perdition, and no way found among us to stay the woe, or stop the carnage, but we must stand aloof, and see our brethren die, and noble ones [of the ministry] with hearts discouraged give up the work for life."[32]

It was this discouragement and lack of support that defeated many ministers in this as in every period. In 1877, Thomas Munnell, acting as secretary for the American Christian Missionary Society, issued a call for a minister to serve in a church in a western state and promised a mission salary of about $700 a year. He was so overwhelmed by the number responding that he was alarmed. He said those offering to go included many of "our best men." He seemed disturbed that so many would feel that they might not be employed where they were through the remainder of the year.

Because of this, he made an open reply in the *Standard*[33] to all unemployed, or partially employed, ministers, advising them, "if you want to do a good work": *First,* take a weak congregation. There are many that can pay $500 a year. This would not be enough to live on, he says, but farmers will probably add enough supplies to make it possible. *Second,* take a country church and add nearby churches to fill the circuit. *Third,* keep off the railroads, go to the interior counties where preachers are more appreciated and more sorely needed. The "railroad churches," he said, really have no need for preachers because they have all the "volunteer preaching" they can use from those who just drop by.

D. R. Dungan gave a picture of the situation in an article entitled "A Change of Preachers" written in 1873. He pointed to the "folly and devastation" of changing preachers so frequently, as the churches seemed to be doing. These unnecessary changes he felt were caused: *first,* by the lack of investigation of ministers who were employed by congregations to fill their pulpits by "trial sermons" or a "week or two" of protracted meetings; *second,* by dissatisfactions brought unduly and unethically into the congregation by visiting preachers who pretended to be the friend of the pastor but brought injury upon him; *third,* by jealousy of other church officers, usually the elders; *fourth,* by lack of moral and spiritual stamina on the part of the preachers; *fifth,* conflict with low moral standards existing in the congregation prior to the pastor's coming and of which he was unaware; and *sixth,* by hypocritical dickering upon salary. He added, "A man who is mentally and spiritually qualified to preach the gospel, ought to find the locality to which he is adapted; and the church employing him should keep him during life."[34] This is one of the earliest statements concerning the need for longer pastorates.

In the *Christian Standard* issues of 1873, men like Thomas Butler[35] speak of the difficult days through which the nation is passing and how it is affecting the preacher. William Powell[36] in West Virginia that year reports that "hundreds of gospel preachers" have had "to turn from the field" to support themselves and their families otherwise. George P. Slade[37] pointed out the evils that were arising because of secular support of the ministry, saying, "May God enable us to trust His ordained means, and while preaching the gospel, look to it for our support." In the 1870's there was also arising a conflict between the so called "young preachers" and the "old preachers." Older men were being replaced by younger men, both as popular traveling evangelists and pastors. This created more tension.

As early as 1869 the older men of the movement were finding themselves worn out in the ministry (unable to keep on the move) and without support. Proposals were offered from time to time on how to care for them, such as offerings from churches they previously had served, or permitting older men to assist in the pastoral work without preaching but with some compensation. All of these proposals failed and by the middle 1870's many state and district assem-

blies of Disciples "lifted" an offering for the "old veterans."
A committee was appointed by the General Convention for
ministerial relief in 1873, but it was not until 1895 when a
layman, A. M. Atkinson, stirred Disciples into action, or-
ganizing the antecedent of the Pension Fund. Its resources
were negligible.

An 1892 editorial in the *Christian Standard* described the
plight of the old minister and attempted to answer the question "How do you account for it?" The writer said, that
for eight decades the minds and energies of both congregations and ministers had been consumed in other matters,
so that "When at length (the old minister) past into the
period of inefficiency, although he was morally entitled to
his "pension," it is clear that no *one* of the numerous
churches previously served by him was bound to *provide*
that "pension" in the absence . . . of any systematic arrangement."[38]

The matter of securing a preacher was left entirely in
the hands of the local congregation, more specifically the
local elders. The journals are full of cries of churches that
had been hurt by itinerant evangelists, often called "vaga-
bonds." There was rapidly developing a group who prized
the name, "Evangelist," but who were religious sensa-
tionalists, "hit and run artists" who made the located ministry their chief target. The traveling and shifting nature of
their work and condition made them vulnerable to all sorts
of immorality.

B. W. Johnson writing in *The Evangelist* in April of 1870
said:

> I have known preachers who would leave home, without
> deigning to inform their family when they would return,
> or upon the other hand, would promise that they would be
> back in a day or two, break their word and be away for
> weeks, without a word in the meantime to relieve the
> anxiety of the lonely wife.[39]

There were a number of these preachers given to occasional imbibing and strong drink. They were sometimes paid in homemade "spirits" which was a common medium of exchange across the frontier. It was said concerning one who preached very well but lived very shoddily that when he was out of the pulpit it was a shame he should ever go in; and when in the pulpit it was a shame he should ever come out.

An editorial in the *Christian Standard* under the title "Is There No Remedy?" presented a case as late as 1890, saying:

> An able preacher in a Southern State has been in the habit of getting very drunken and remaining in this condition for days and nights. When discovered, he confesses and is forgiven and goes on preaching. Recently he was imprisoned in one of his drunken debauches. The matter was brought up at the State Convention and many of the preachers present were inclined to sit in judgement on him forthwith, and publish him, and refuse him any recognition. And who could blame them? They were filled with righteous indignation. . . . But the question arose: Is it the province of a State Convention to deal with the standing of a minister? It was suggested that the local church in which he held membership should deal with him, not the convention. This view was finally accepted. But it was found that he held membership in a far away congregation which he rarely visited. This congregation knows little about him and perhaps cares less. And so the matter is allowed to take its course.[40]

He cited other cases of "rapid removal" of such preachers and observed, "the independency of the church may be carried to a ruinous length. In the name of sacred right, let us have a clean ministry even if we have to call in the police!"

But on the other hand some felt the minister to be most distrusted was the well-educated. They preferred the self-educated with a gift toward quoting chapter and verse and only understanding the English Bible.

Responding to this in 1872, W. K. Pendleton said,

"(Campbell) neither conceived, nor approved, any short hand methods of manufacturing ministers, but rather deplored the thought that the idea of an educated Christian ministry, the supply of which formed so large a part of his purpose in founding Bethany College, should be degraded by any such inadequate expedient."[41] But by the turn of the century, Bible Colleges which made no serious attempt at the general liberal education Campbell advocated, came on the scene to satisfy the demand for quick education in "first principles." A practical type of presbyterial control over the ministry was reflected by B. U. Watkins, writing regarding this need in the *Christian Standard* in 1888:

> Very early in the current Reformation, a very talented and successful preacher was proved guilty of serious immorality. It seemed like an awful thing, in our infant brotherhood, to silence an able and successful evangelist. And as he had confessed his sin, promised reformation, some influential brethren thought he ought to continue preaching. But others of equal intelligence insisted he should be silenced. But, to prevent division, the case was referred to Alexander Campbell. He decided that the offender should be silenced. It is now many years since I read the decision; but to the best of my memory Mr. Campbell argues something like this: Confession and reformation may restore such a sinner to a private membership in the church and it should be considered a great favor that such a transgressor could be saved on any conditions whatever. But it will never do to intrust the honor of the gospel of Christ to the hands of one who had wickedly betrayed that trust, and disgraced his holy calling.[42]

While this decision may have contributed much to the thinking of men like Mr. Watkins and others, the method of making such a decision disappeared with the first generation under the cries for absolute freedom of the congregation and the minister. It is very apparent to the careful student of our history that the first generation, with its Campbells, Scotts and Stones, was far more presbyterial and episcopal in its views than the second or third.

Many of us think a ministerial placement registry was something that Willard Wickizer devised a couple of decades ago, but as a matter of fact, Thomas Munnell operated one, listing churches seeking preachers and preachers seeking churches in the 1870's.[43] Neither Munnell, or, for that matter, anyone following him, has been able to solve this matter of placement or that of ministerial support. Stating the problem and calling for more "laborers," Errett editoralized in the *Christian Standard* in 1888: "We need thousands of pious, consecrated young men—not thousand dollar men, but three, four and five-hundred-dollar men. There are school teachers in all districts, doctors and lawyers in all villages—workers in all fields, except the Master's field. Can it be that Christian workers are more mercenary than any other? Can the poor—poor communities—be taught and physicked, but cannot the gospel be preached to them because they *are* poor?"[44] That statement and question was addressed to preachers.

Later he had this word for congregations: "We verily believe that many Christian people cherish the idea that poverty is a help to piety so far as ministers of the gospel are concerned. Many a congregation is wonderfully careful that its pastor shall not be hindered with any load of riches. But they who serve at the altar have a right to living from the altar. This is the divine order of affairs, and to keep a minister in abject poverty is as unrighteous as it is wrong."[45]

It was becoming crystal clear that stewardship in the churches of the Campbell-Stone Movement had been hurt more by the needless continuance of the "tent-making" ministry than any other factor. The parsimonious church member was always asking, "Why is it necessary to contribute, that a minister spend more time in pastoring the flock and proclaiming the gospel, when we can have the services of 'Farmer Smith,' or 'Teacher Brown' at half the cost." In a generous mood, some argued that more could be given to missions and benevolences, if part-time ministers were used. But the result of all of this was invariably the opposite. At the close of the nineteenth century financial support for all causes, including the ministry was sinking. O. G. White, one of our pastors who is still living, having past the century mark this fall, wrote a book more than fifty years ago under the title *Ministering the Word of God.* He spoke of this period in which much had been said "against the salary of the modern pastor," but, he contended, the New Testament advises that it is proper to pay the man who "gives himself fully to the word."[46]

In 1890, J. K. Speer sized up the proposition of objection to pastors as being primarily a matter of just being born in the objectionable mood; he said, "among the 'I object' class are found a number of ministers who oppose salaried preachers, yet they always demand big pay for protracted meetings. . . . A congregation employs a preacher and a no-pay, no pray, member cries out, 'I object,' and proceeds to hunt up means for destroying the pastor." He adds that others in a similar mood object to the education of ministers. Then he concludes, "Give me the congregation with its God fearing and able pastor, who is beloved and supported on an equal footing with the membership, and I will show you 'Ancient Christianity restored.' "[47]

Others began to see that church organization and the lack of proper relationship between the officers of the church was threatening the church's mission and its ministry. W. T. Moore wrote:

We should, therefore, in the light of modern thinking, and modern development, seek for an irenicon which will do away with the endless jargon concerning "Historic Episcopacy," the "Credal Presbytery," and the "Congregational Conference." As a matter of fact there are no hard and fast lines taught in the New Testament concerning church organization.

He goes on to say that this does not mean that organization is not necessary, for it is. He adds, "undoubtedly the church organization found in the New Testament *is not* in harmony with the organization of modern times. It is probably safe to say that the New Testament Churches were Episcopal, Presbyterian and Congregational, rather than one of these to the exclusion of the others."[48] Others such as Frederick Kershner and Will Robinson have later joined him in this view finding the seeds of all church polities in the New Testament.

Some of our ministers at the end of the nineteenth century were handicapped by their attitudes. J. H. Garrison regularly warned these of the "blight of sectarian narrowness, Pharisaic legalism, that contents itself with propagating its own peculiarities, while giving no emphasis to the common faith."[49] For many, debate was so precious, with its exhileration of public speaking, the headiness of it all, and the temptation to "win" at any cost even with slight misrepresentations of the opponent's view. This kept driving the doctrinal wedges deeper and deeper both within the brotherhood and with other parts of the body of Christ. The temptation for this sort of thing seemed irresistible. Fragmentation followed.

Yet there were scores of unheralded men responding and giving themselves completely to the cause with great breadth of spirit. One wrote, "There is no more sacred calling than that of a preacher of the gospel. He stands between people and God, not as a priest or advocate, but as the herald of salvation. For this reason every legitimate means should be used to impress upon his mind the responsibility and importance of his position."[50] Really the remarkable thing is that they accomplished so much against the handicaps of lack of esteem, lack of support, lack of education, lack of encouragement, as well as lack of mutual concern.

So, for the nineteenth century as this century, though the proposition of no artificial distinction between preachers and laymen was, and is, valid, practical matters arose from this which resulted in a narrow conception both of the

Christian ministry *and* the Christian laity. For the most part it hinged upon the eldership. There was the tendency to overemphasize the right of the layman to perform the priestly functions of the church, and at the same time to under-emphasize the responsibility of both the layman and the ordained minister to carry forth the tasks of teaching and pastoral care. Occasionally, the minister who cherished freedom found himself bound to the narrow limitations attached to his work, sometimes self-imposed, sometimes imposed by his congregation.

The mention of a "sometimes deacon" brought smiles to some faces at the outset of this chapter. These may have been prompted by the thought of some carefree deacons whose sporadic activity is scarcely worthy of any position. But I have a theory that I think is supportable. It is that the attitude of the church and the Christian toward this humble office will largely determine their concept of ministry and that of the church of the future.

As with elders, there is some work for deacons that is rarely done today, because those holding the offices have not been instructed in it. Most people who downgrade the deacon's work have never done it, nor seriously considered it. Substantial thoughts of ministry can, and do, arise when counting and posting offerings, washing the communion glasses, assisting the baptismal candidates or teaching children and youth which sometimes deacons do, for elders most often are reserved for adults, if they teach at all. In all these tasks, however simple, lies the opportunity to explore spiritual depths equal to any theological profundity as well as to participate in Christian service to a degree not possible elsewhere in the church.

To be a *diakonos*—a deacon—is to be a servitor and that means constant employment in the Lord's task; to be a deacon is to work and that is liturgical in the basic sense of that word; to be a deacon is to be an attendant and that means there is something and someone to tend; to be a deacon is to give and that is stewardship; to be a deacon is to be a helper and that means love; to be a deacon is to be a caretaker and that word means sensitivity to need; to be a deacon is to be a servant and to be a servant is to minister. No one can be a minister who does not know first that he is a deacon.

Many years have passed since I heard W. R. Walker give a series of lectures on the ministry. Fortunately, they were later published. Having been a part of the nineteenth century ministry, he spoke with some authority on the best of that ministry of the Campbell-Stone Movement as he knew it then. He said:

> The work of ministering (is revealed) to be the highest, holiest, most blessed calling of God to man. It entrusts to the minister the introduction of his fellows into covenant relations with God, with their cultural progress, and their guidance in religious activities and true Christian living. There is almost a hint in the Bible that angels envied men this glorious task. The responsibilities of it are sobering. The honor is sufficient. The rewards are abiding. In all the world, there is no area in which men serve that is comparable to that of the Christian ministry.[51]

That was the case two generations ago and many find it to be the case today.

NOTES

1. H. K. Shaw, *Hoosier Disciples* (Indianapolis: The Bethany Press for the Association of Christian Churches in Indiana, 1966), pp. 144-145.
2. B. K. Smith, *The Scriptural Organization* (Indianapolis: Indianapolis Printing and Publishing House, 1871), p. 72.
3. *Ibid.,* pp. 63-66.
4. John Knox, "The Ministry in the Primitive Church," *The Ministry in Historical Perspectives,* edited by H. R. Niebuhr and D. D. Williams (New York: Harper and Brothers, 1956), pp. 8-25, See p. 21 especially.
5. D. E. Stevenson, "Ordained Disciples Elders: A Brief Historical Review," *The Scroll,* Vol. LVIII (Autumn, 1960), p. 20.
6. F. D. Kershner, *The Restoration Handbook* (Cincinnati: Standard Publishing Company, 1918), p. 13.
7. M. M. Davis, *The Eldership* (Cincinnati: The Standard Publishing Co., 1912), p. 46.

8. J. C. Stark, *The King and His Kingdom*, Part II, *Church Organization* (Hamilton, Ill.: Published by the author, 1902), p. 316.
9. *Ibid.*, pp. 320-321.
10. Ben Franklin, Editorial Correspondence, *Christian Standard* (September 21, 1872), p. 298.
11. A. Campbell, *The Christian System*, p. 84.
12. H. G. Goodykoontz, *The Minister in Reformed Tradition*, p. 65.
13. Moses E. Lard, "The Work of the Past—The Symptoms of the Future," *Lards Quarterly*, Vol. II, No. 3 (April, 1865), pp. 251-262.
14. Editorial Correspondence, *Christian Standard* (May 22, 1869), p. 162.
15. Isaac Errett, Editorial, *Christian Standard* (May 8, 1869), p. 146.
16. *Ibid.*, p. 169.
17. Earl I. West, *The Search for the Ancient Order*, Vol. II (Indianapolis: Religious Book Service, 1950), pp. 453-454.
18. *Ibid.*, p. 455.
19. W. W. Hayden, "Position and Authority of Pastor, or Resident Preacher," *Christian Standard* (Sept. 1, 1877), pp. 273 and 274.
20. J. S. Lamar, Editorial, *Christian Standard* (Feb. 5, 1870).
21. Thomas Munnell, *The Care of All the Churches* (St. Louis: Christian Publishing Co., 1878), see Flyleaf and pp. 37 and 102.
22. *Ibid.*, p. 36.
23. *Ibid.*, p. 108.
24. E. V. Zollars, "A Strong Ministry," *Christian Standard* (December 27, 1890), p. 899.
25. F. M. Bruner, A Tract, *The Apostolic Church and the Position of Pastor*, Abingdon, Illinois, 1879.
26. E. I. West, *The Search for the Ancient Order*, Vol. II, p. 109, p. 146.
27. W. E. Garrison, *Religion Follows the Frontier* (New York: Harpers, 1931), p. 31.
28. Thomas Munnell, Editorial Correspondence, *American Christian Review*, Vol. X, No. 27 (July 2, 1867), p. 209.
29. B. W. Johnson, Editorial, *The Evangelist* (Jan. 8, 1880), p. 1, 30.
30. J. C. Stark, *The King and The Kingdom*, p. 296.
31. *Ibid.*, p. 297.
32. *Ibid.*, p. 322.
33. Thomas Munnell, "My Call for a Preacher," *Christian Standard* (Feb. 16, 1877), p. 50.
34. D. R. Dungan, "A Change of Preachers," *The Evangelist* (Aug. 18, 1873), pp. 252-253.
35. T. D. Butler, "Moral Bankruptcy," *Christian Standard* (June 14, 1873), p. 185.
36. Wm. Powell, editorial correspondence, *Christian Standard* (July 21, 1873), p. 258.
37. George P. Slade, editorial correspondence, *Christian Standard* (July 21, 1873), p. 258.
38. Editorial, *Christian Standard* (Aug. 20, 1892), p. 706.
39. B. W. Johnson, Editorial, *The Evangelist* (April 6, 1870), p. 4.
40. Editorial, "Is There No Remedy?" *Christian Standard* (Dec. 20, 1890), p. 878.
41. W. K. Pendleton, "Ministerial Course at Bethany College," *Christian Standard* (Aug. 10, 1872), p. 250.

42. B. U. Watkins, Correspondence, *Christian Standard* (Sept. 1, 1888), p. 551.

43. See announcements in *Christian Standard* beginning May 21, 1870, p. 163 ff.

44. Isaac Errett, "More Laborers," *Christian Standard* (Dec. 15, 1888), p. 806.

45. Isaac Errett, "Poorly Paid Ministers," *Christian Standard* (Sept. 15, 1888), p. 589.

46. O. G. White, *Ministering the Word of God* (St. Louis: Christian Publishing Co., 1916), p. 85.

47. J. K. Speer, "I Object," *Christian Standard* (Aug. 30, 1890), p. 569.

48. W. T. Moore, *Preacher Problems* (New York: Fleming H. Revell Co., 2nd Edition, 1907), pp. 250-251.

49. J. H. Garrison, *The Reformation of the Nineteenth Century*, a tract.

50. Correspondence signed by "A Young Preacher," *Christian Standard* (May 21, 1892), p. 442.

51. W. R. Walker, *A Ministering Ministry* (Cincinnati: The Standard Publishing Co., 1938), p. 120.

III

Changing Ministries for Changing Times

The Christian Church (Disciples of Christ) came as a nineteenth century effort to bring "the unity, peace and purity" of the Church of Christ on Earth, which was to be realized by the repudiation of all written creeds, church courts, hierarchies, and priestcraft. It called for a restoration of the "ancient order of things." It did not call for the elimination of a set-apart ministry, even though at times it may have looked this way.

Environmental changes have come in the present century affecting the Christian ministry with greater rapidity and force than ever before. For those of the Campbell-Stone Movement these have included the end of the American frontier, mobility from five to five hundred, if not fifteen hundred miles per hour, communications shifting from dimly lighted meeting houses and printed words to TV, a factual knowledge explosion doubling and quadrupling each decade, the acceptance of organizations as a fact of life now in all divisions of this movement to some degree, the development of the functional system of congregational organization and the blossoming of the ecumenical movement.

The impact of these upon us is apparent. The span from the optimism of 1845 with its *Millennial Harbinger* to the pessimism of 1945 with its atomic bomb is emotionally, psychologically, socially and culturally *more* than a century. It is two complete ages and the church and the ministry are now in a new age. Whether you read the words from a Jack Meyer[1] of the Church of Christ group or a Dudley Strain[2] writing for the Committee on the Ministry of the Home and State Missions Planning Council of the Disciples the implications are about the same. Approve or not, there is developing a professional ministry with its own standards, its code of ethics, its tests and measurements. Meyer presents a "Scriptural basis" for a "full time and church supported ministry;" which would have been unheard of in the halls of David Lipscomb College a generation ago. He explains that:

> With all of the elders usually employed in secular work and unable to give full time to the church they usually look to the preacher for much executive work.[3]

This "pastoral director" is the common denominator of American Protestantism. How to be one, and be effective, is what Strain's and Meyer's books are all about.

There has now developed within this communion, in the course of these one hundred and sixty years, an order of ministry, largely following the reformed tradition. The relationships between congregations, lay officers and employed ministry have not been explicitly defined. They are, nevertheless, generally understood. It is true that there is no hierarchical authority. The Campbell-Stone Movement cannot rightly claim full credit for this achievement, since this was the declared aim of the reformation of the sixteenth and seventeenth century.

All along we have seen in the Campbell-Stone Movement a field always "white unto the harvest" as far as unmet needs for ministry are concerned. Yet, there has existed almost from the beginning a considerable number of laborers (ministers) ready to serve who were not fully used. The reason generally was they were not adequately supported, or prepared, or that they found themselves engaged in other activities which kept them from public ministry.

Thus, these practical matters, more than the arguments against the "status," or "hireling," ministry, handicapped them both at home and abroad. It encouraged their prejudices against the city and kept them out of the metropolitan areas. One could hardly live off the land there! And many were so supported. Thus this movement developed a free, but also only partially employed, ministry. This freedom they cherished. Generally they were determined, above all, to be individually free; secondly, to be committed to their Lord and, finally, committed to one another. It rarely occurred to anyone that these priorities might ever conflict.

For the brotherhood, the general view was that *any* effective evangelist, or minister, worth his salt, should be able to go into a new field, capture it with the primitive gospel, and find support there. This system worked remarkably well in Frontier America. Factors in its success should not be lost. Chief among these is the matter of putting the responsibility upon the people most intimately involved. For example, when Oklahoma was settled, though claims were staked for congregations in the Cherokee Strip by a representative of the Board of Church Extension, each congregation had to develop the church there with little or no outside aid. Groups of Disciples moved into the territory together and stayed near one another in order to continue fellowships which had begun earlier in Missouri, Kansas or Texas. Some other denominations with larger home mission funds were not nearly so successful.

At the dawn of the twentieth century when it should have been apparent there would be a more settled and erudite society, the leaders of the Campbell-Stone Movement were not necessarily looking for ways to improve the educational and moral qualifications of their ministry. Proselyting, quick indoctrination, and "catch as catch can" methods were too successful. Bible Colleges were launched, which did not offer the classical and liberal education that a century before the founders of this movement had considered so essential. Even a third of the way through the present century, Disciples had not yet an accredited seminary and many of their colleges had lowered standards for ministerial education.

I do not mean to say that there were no individually well prepared men to come through this system in the early nineteen-hundreds. There were many. The commitment of individual ministers, particularly the pastors, at the turn of the century was as great or greater than ever.

My own father was typical. He spent seven years in academies, Bible Colleges, colleges and seminaries, though he earned no more than a Bachelor's Degree. He handled Greek better than many seminary graduates and supplemented his education with rather extensive reading in all fields of knowledge in true American style. He organized several congregations and baptized over three thousand persons from 1908 to 1954. A generation ago he was one of the better known ministers in Kansas. Yet, his largest salary was $60 a week and parsonage. Somehow, mother and he managed to rear seven of us on this. Just how they managed, I do not fully understand. Yet, being the oldest, I do recall that there was always *at least* one cow, a calf or a pig to fatten, a flock of chickens both for eggs and meat and a large garden to hoe. Present health laws would not permit such agricultural practices within city limits!

Dad was always employed in the wheat harvest and at times both he and mother taught school and/or participated in similar enterprises to bolster the sagging budget. I am confident that all of this was not due to my father's varied interests. It was a necessity. This was the way a Kansas congregation expected its "preacher" to make it, particularly if he was so inconsiderate as to want a large family and to burden the parsonage with the same. Though there were plenty of others, I have used him as an example, because I do not want to embarrass anyone. The Smith situation was a typical situation.

Behind all this self-support was the idea that *anyone* could perform this ministry. It was nice, but not necessary, to have additional education. If one had it, he was to enjoy it for its own value alone. The idea for support was—let there be general participation in the agricultural enterprise! Laymen weren't joking when they talked about the pastor working "only one day a week." Not really!

With it all, the temptation for the pastor was to leave and take to the field of evangelism, because there was more financial support there. Indeed, it was the twentieth century traveling evangelist who, for the most part, destroyed the image that Campbell had held for this office. Commercialism in evangelism, of the most sordid sort, came into play in the eighteen-nineties and the first two decades of this century.

F. D. Kershner put it mildly when he observed in 1919:

Lately, . . . there has been a tendency to adopt some of the uncertain methods of the very 'evangelism' which the New Testament records discountenance, and as a result our message has oft-times been shorn of its power.[4]

But in 1919 all "orthodox" congregations, expecting to overcome the "errors of the sects," planned at least one annual "revival". An evangelistic party in the 1920's was out-of-date if it did not come equipped with plenty side-show entertainment, including a variety of musical instruments, chalk artists, catchy jingles and campaign schemes. The evangelist was then the highest paid preacher in the Movement and often his methods at fund raising for these special efforts blighted and blunted any attempt at genuine and consistent stewardship thereafter in the congregation.

The result, many people developed a cynicism toward the "vested" interest of evangelistic preaching and the evangelistic preacher. Though some Campbell-Stone advocates have justified "crowd-getters" from Cane Ridge to the twentieth century municipal auditorium, today it takes a Hollywood performer plus prime TV time to accomplish what three or four decades ago could have been effected by renting a good hall and posting a few handbills. Though today some still try, by and large, the traveling evangelist is gone. From several hundred evangelists in 1920, fewer than thirty-five are listed in the current Disciple Year Book. While many Church of Christ congregations call their resident preachers, "evangelists," in newspaper advertisements and church signs, today they are really settled. By 1910, virtually every church of Disciples having regular preaching, had a man on the field and, according to studies made in 1925, eighty-five percent lived in parsonages.[6]

Older men began to run into more and more trouble. Salary studies in 1925 indicated a sharp decline for the support of ministers after they attain age 55; and at 65, their compensation averaged the same as at the beginning of their ministries.[7] Many of these men found it increasingly difficult to support themselves and some of their circumstances were tragic.

Young preachers were sought everywhere to draw young people. Oldsters, too young for retirement, but not youthful enough for congregations believing them to be liabilities, remain today the larger number of unemployed—or partially employed—ministers. Only once in this century, and that during World War II, when hundreds of our ministers were in military service, have all been fully employed.

The dominant Disciple concept of church administration during our time has been, "find out what the people want and do it." Or to put it another way: "let's vote!" Many more Christian Churches have guilt feelings over not having a "contest" in each election of elders and deacons than neglecting to determine whether those nominated are qualified. A church I know sets in form type the phrase, *"democratically elected,"* to drop it in such sentences as, "the

Nominating Committee—*democratically elected*—shall receive nominations from the congregation for elders, deacons
and deaconesses, who shall be—*democratically elected*—
etc." I do not mean to speak disparagingly of the democratic
processes. I mention it here to illustrate the defensiveness
of our people for *this concern to the exclusion of all others.*

A year ago *The Christian* published some "polls" used by
pulpit committees to sample congregational attitudes on
what they preferred in a minister.[8] They ran the range from
what his weight should be to how much education he should
have. Indeed, they would be amusing, if they did not mirror
tragic misunderstandings regarding the ministry. Most of
their questions emphasized the truth that "to be a minister
is to be a servant," but they failed to direct the church into
its joint ministry (or servanthood). They implied a prevailing notion of the 'hired man' concept with no mention of
prophetic, and little of priestly, or pastoral, responsibilities.
The tragic result has been the "pressure to please" at *all*
cost by some pastors. It is something like running for office
weekly! The consequences are generally short pastorates.
Two extensive studies[9] show the average to be less than
three years for churches reporting to the Disciple Yearbook.
It is barely possible that some long pastorates do not establish any better rapport for mutual ministry than the short
ones. If they represent a form of "benevolent dictatorship",
certainly not.

Today "trial sermons" are generally frowned upon, since
most self-respecting ministers will not knowingly participate in such contests. Though thoroughly outlined by commissions on the ministry and in publications of a national
committee, the established ethical procedures to "call" a
minister are often rejected by a practical minded pulpit
committee. They know the finance committee wants a ministerial contract that "sits well" with the chief supporters
and which can be terminated in emergencies more easily.

I do not want to indulge in any maudlin sentimentalism

for the minister. I would not be patronizing or paternalistic. I would not shed great tears in his behalf. He doesn't want this either individually, or collectively! He knows that such sentimentality is not a sign of warm-heartedness. Nothing weeps so copiously as a cake of ice in the noon day sun!

But I must speak of modern concepts. Not *all* people and *all* congregations among us fit this pattern, but far too many do. Here is a pastor who has served a congregation for a decade and a half, who in the eyes of some is losing his effectiveness. The elders meet for a couple of nights and invite all the dissidents to bring charges against him. He is not present to answer. On the third night the official board hears the recommendation of the elders to terminate the services of the minister. They are narrowly supported. The pastor decides not to "fight", in order to avoid a church division. When the chief elder and board chairman calls one not of their number to ask him how to set up a pulpit committee and in return is asked if they have consulted the state secretary, the innocent reply is, "state secretary, who is he?" The tone of this question emits both the ignorance and astonishment that any other elder—or elders—outside the local congregation might be concerned with this church or its ministry. This attitude is foreign to the New Testament! The example I have given is a real one, and is of a church in the cooperative and liberal tradition.

More than one minister has returned from summer vacation to find this transaction has taken place. That it occurs in all three wings of the Campbell-Stone communion, I think is quite apparent. As a matter of fact, my actuarial orientation for average ages, *and* survival, causes me to look over any ministerial group quite carefully. I have attended many North American Convention assemblies and a few Church of Christ gatherings. I note that there are even fewer gray and bald heads among these than among the Disciples. Hence, I conclude that the "dropouts" there run proportionately higher than among Disciples. There are other evidences supporting my conclusion. The dropout rate among the Disciples is almost two in ten after seminary, and/or the completion of the second pastorate.[10]

The general attitude in the face of this on the part of some is a speculative aloofness. Privately you hear ambivalent expressions of sympathy for the individual who has been "displaced", accompanied by pious declarations that the law of the survival of the fittest is God's way of "winnowing the chaff" from the ministry. And, of course, the ministry must be protected both ways. There are about as many men who should be counseled out of the ministry as counseled into it, but that should occur earlier than this, at least by the first year of seminary.

Aloofness, more specific than speculative, also is heard from some fellow ministers who say, "this never happened to me". But neither type of aloofness is an answer. The system that breeds this sort of thing goes on and on. One need not be opposed to congregationalism in order to cry out for more responsible congregations.

In the midst of this there has been some attention to the minister's dilemma. Much of the discussion has been around theological propositions. A great cry has again risen against clericalism and institutionalism. Many of our young men have picked up this cry from scholars whose background is the European scene, the established church and a status ministry. It is amazing and amusing to see these chaps apply this to the Campbell-Stone Movement. One wonders how they escaped the knowledge that these were the battles of our fathers. But if you enjoy fighting straw men and raising dead issues, as many Disciples do, who is to deny these lads? Let us only observe that somehow in some places church history is either not taught, or is avoided, or, if taught, is out of date.

Practically, one would like to see all communions give a bit more attention to the realities which face both the minister and the church in the current situation. Shorter hours for parishioners, for example, generally means longer hours for the minister. Believe me, there is much he *cannot* put into a pastoral report be it to the official board *or* the elders. That which is left out is both the great and the small— but the heart of a servant ministry: the unheralded gift (perhaps the last dollar he had) which he gave to some poor fellow in need, the long night of mediating a family quarrel which ended in failure, the pleasant smile and light-hearted exchange given a constantly complaining church officer, the loneliness that genuine ministerial ethics impose, the courage to stay with a people who are beyond their depth in social change, the willingness to go on when being "dumped" for the same reason, the stamina to keep on serving in youth conferences and the like when he is past fifty, the anguish in the parsonage as son or daughter falls below expectations bringing nasty criticism and an unexpected move, the heart breaking disappointment in church folk who can't be counted on, the hard battle with personal pride, the humility represented in the genuine dignity with which any great ministry is carried, and ultimately the acceptance of a retirement where he may be forgotten. This is the life of the twentieth century minister.

If he is prophetic in his preaching, he is sure to be plagued with wee hour threatening phone calls and anonymous mail. If he is overly efficient as a pastor-administrator he may find himself hemmed in with impossible tasks. Daily it may mean new crosses, but most men, who are committed, face them without complaint. In the ministry, they expect to make sacrifices. It is hypocritical, however, when such are made either without conviction, or without the sharing of a concerned congregation and the church as a whole.

In fact, the "loner" who makes sacrifices regularly without involving the church and its people may not really be a martyr, he may simply be suffering from a complex. Maturity is coming rapidly to those men in the Campbell-Stone Movement today who see their involvement both with a total church and a total ministry of which they are a part.

In the knowledge of such an undertaking can we not lay aside our inaccurate, emotional labels of one another and declare a moratorium on issues that have long since passed? Today, with missiles poised, bombs now loaded on rockets, well aimed and able to wipe out all mankind, with law and order breaking down within the hearts and minds of men, our nation threatened with civil disorders of all sorts, while the acceptance of the gospel is on the decline, I ask how can we possibly go on separating ourselves over the things we do? How can we allow ourselves the pretention of living in two separate "worlds", (one religious and the other secular)? How can we intelligently hold Christ as our guide and Alexander Campbell as our mentor and propose such as this?

We have no choice, as I see it, but to confront the conditions of our time. The first of these conditions is that both the church and the ministry have lost esteem. We should have known this was coming, because no persecution is as subtle or deadly, as public acceptance and personal denial. This is the experience of the ministry in the past few decades. The easiest way to dismiss the relevancy of the church and the gospel is to insist that every public gathering be opened with prayer by a clergyman, but deny him the right to speak upon any issue.

That is the situation for the twentieth century minister. T. J. Mullen observes:

> There is a growing attitude of anti-clericalism in America today . . . . There may have been a time when the typical pastor was a symbol of deep dedication, self-sacrifice and hard working humility. However, that image is held by fewer people today than in the past.[11]

Eugene Boring of Phillips University's Graduate Seminary describes the current situation accurately when he

says that the present status of the minister is like that
mournful word of the Old Testament, "Ichabod," which
means "the glory has departed." He observed that in:

> the last century it was a matter of some "glory" to be a
> minister. To read the life of Thomas Campbell, for instance,
> is to behold a man . . . whose moving to another community
> was felt to be a public loss. . . . Not so long ago Raymond
> Calkins could write a book called *Romance of the Ministry*,
> and Edgar DeWitt Jones could entitle his history of the
> Yale Lectures on Preaching, *The Royalty of the Pulpit*.
> Parents held up the ministry to their children as among the
> most noble of vocations. . . . Today? Well, "the parson" is a
> cartoon figure from the past. A book entitled *Romance of
> the Ministry* is likely to be taken as a story about a cleric
> and his secretary. Though the greatness of the men of the
> Yale Lectures and of their historian is not to be denied, that
> was another time, and in our day we find it difficult to get
> "royalty" and "pulpit" into the same phrase. And parents
> tremble at the possibility that their son might turn down
> the engineering scholarship to go to seminary.[12]

But, under God, all of this should *not* cause us to lose
heart. In these times there are good signs, too; signs of
hope and signs of promise! In this century they have come
in six identifiable areas for Disciple ministers.

One has been *recruitment*. In the late 1900's Disciples
recruited many of their ministers from other denominations. Half the Disciple preachers of Indiana in the eighteen
seventies had been so recruited.[13] By the turn of the century
it began to look to its own. The call of the mission field at
home and abroad, echoed in the "Men and Millions Movement" prior to World War I, enlisted more than a thousand.
Participation in other interdenominational efforts, such as
the Student Volunteer Movement and Christian Endeavor
brought others. By the second decade of this century, recruitment was carried on in youth camps and conferences
which led to the enlistment of scores. Following World War
II during the "Crusade for a Christian World" the specific

goal for recruitment was more nearly reached than many others.

So successful was this recruitment, that there was justifiable doubt as to whether the church would respond with sufficient support to send those volunteering into the world's fields. There was also a growing concern as to whether some volunteers were qualified. Scientific tests were devised, based on the experiences of educational, industrial institutions, and other denominations to determine the aptitude and adaptability of the recruit for the ministry.

While this procedure was not widely accepted by the churches, it did emphasize the need for upgrading the ministry for the demanding task in an urban and urbane society. Perhaps the most verified conclusion from these efforts was a general acknowledgment that a program of recruitment based on psychological guidance and testing, however valid, may give an accurate profile of personality, but does not necessarily provide motivation, or direction, to the ministry.

By 1958, Disciples were seeing the possibility of greatly enlarged numbers in the ministry. Many Disciples were prophesying a doubling of seminary enrollment in the decade of the sixties which would have quadrupled the number of prepared leaders for this brotherhood. Only the forces of a society absorbed with its own secularism and war reversed this trend.

Allan Sharp of Atlantic Christian College is right in his analysis of the current shortage, I believe. He urges us to quit making excuses and to recognize the reasons for the deficiency which lie within the church itself, due largely to what he describes as the recruitment factor, the economic factor and the educational factor. He points out that, "There is more glamour and publicity for those who explore outer space than for those who probe inner space."[14]

Perhaps, the world is going so fast these days that the cry is for a pilot, not a preacher. But one can't help but feel that our time calls for more dedication, both in the ministry and from those who will support adequate leadership. The fact is, our present recruitment problem is created by our inability to invite young men and women to join in a dangerous, challenging and exciting venture for Christ where they can expect the genuine concern and support of the whole church. Because of our uncertainty in regard to the latter, we cannot, or do not, make this call. There is little challenge to extend *without* the promise of common commitment and support.

A *second* area of change has been *ministerial education.* Beginning this century with no accredited seminaries of their own, Disciples now have four; all equipped with new campuses and buildings erected since World War II; all with well equipped faculties and fine libraries; all sufficiently ecumenically oriented that they prepare almost as many ministers for other denominations as their own. In addition, Disciples participate in a score of other seminaries, either contributing students or faculty, and in some cases, financial support.

For the group, styled by A. T. DeGroot, "Church of Christ Number Two," the number of Bible colleges has grown beyond count. So, it is possible that the Campbell-Stone Movement offers more opportunity at ministerial education now than in any time in its history.

This century's *third* area of change has been in the matter of *ordination.* Most congregations now acknowledge that a person set apart for public ministry is not merely the concern of a single congregation and one group of elders. Though this was recognized in their first convention in 1849, Disciples did not get far along this line until a century later, when commissions on the ministry, presently localized in states and areas, came into being.

One of the most effective advocates of such was F. E. Davison. Speaking before a special assembly on ordination held prior to the 1936 San Antonio Convention, he said,

"If our friends of the Pension Fund are successful in awakening our churches to a new respect and love for the ministry, then it behooves us to do all in our power to see to it that those who seek ordination are worthy of the high calling."[15] Later the convention appointed a committee which suggested four minimum standards for candidates. These were: (1) moral character and temperamental fitness, (2) demonstration of ability to think clearly, being so recommended by his educators, (3) demonstration of ability to preach with power, evangelize and be a pastor (perhaps in an apprenticeship), (4) demonstration of preparation by submitting to the proper committee a written sermon which "reflects his passion and objectives for the Christian Ministry".[15]

While the appointment of the committee brought a storm of argument in the brotherhood journals, and the standards on ordination were not immediately adopted, the door was opened for serious consideration in 1948 and 1963 when more definitive action was taken by the International Convention. And out of this effort came both a "code of ethics" to which many Disciple ministers subscribe and an almost universal acceptance of state commissions on the ministry. These commissions offered opportunities to ordinands to be examined by them, and local congregations began almost immediately to use them and invited the addition of their endorsement to that of local elders. Today most commissions are composed of both laymen and ministers. The candidate is usually encouraged to wait until he has completed seminary before expecting ordination. His progress is checked on from time to time and needed encouragement is given. The commission also may "license" student ministers who need such documents in certain states in order to perform various ministerial functions.

Under the title, *In Christ's Place*, a significant book by Dean Ronald Osborn of Christian Theological Seminary, had just come from the press. It is perhaps the most scholarly to be produced by any of the Campbell-Stone Movement on the Biblical doctrines of ministry. Osborn helps us see that, though from the first century, baptism has meant ordination into the common and mutual ministry of the church, the New Testament itself does not use the verbs of *"appointment to office"* for believers in general with but one striking exception, and that is in the majestic anthem of praise to the Lamb in the Apocalypse. Even there, it refers to the ransomed from every tribe and nation being "ordained" as a priest of God. Elsewhere, Osborn observes, these verbs are used exclusively for ordaining to office in the church. And, though it is God who most frequently is the subject of setting one apart for the ministry, the church also ordains. He concludes:

> Ordination means corporate appointment to the public ministry of the gospel. The church's action in such appointment represents its faithful effort to discern and to recognize the ordaining work of God.
>
> By ordination, the church grants corporate acknowledgment to its public servants.
>
> In the act of ordination the church entrusts its public ministers with particular duties and pledges them its faithful support.
>
> By prayer and the laying on of hands the church seeks for its ministers the divine gifts needed for the faithful exercise of their servanthood under Christ.[16]

Osborn adds,

> The ordering of the church expresses its wholeness, for it shares the responsibility for corporate faithfulness. And when we act to set apart an order of ministers, we do not dilute the holiness of the church, but rather enhance it.[17]

On the other hand, there are other Disciples who state that even the words, "order of the ministry", so easily acceptable a century ago in Campbell's *Christian System,* are "distinct from and in contrast to the priesthood of all believers" and "takes away from local congregations their vital and significant responsibility and privileges concerning the ministry."[18] Such criticism was leveled in 1849 and again in 1936 for standards for ordination. It was Barton Hunter, then, who charged that these proposals would "lead" to the "destruction of local church autonomy."[19]

However, Biblical studies beginning with Campbell's *Christian System,* and amplified by such men as Will Robinson, F. D. Kershner and others, would lead us to agree that:

> The conclusion is inescapable. Within the corporate ministry of praise to God and service to man in which all Christians participate by their membership in the body, the Apostolic church established a constellation of offices or ministries which it laid upon persons it considered qualified to exercise them. Without derogating from the servanthood of the whole body, without implications of sacerdotalism or hierarchy, that church regarded these persons as particularly deserving the title, "ministers" or "servants."[20]

The *fourth* development has been that of the state secretary-minister in the matter of *ministerial placement.* While the brotherhood has developed a national registry for the circulation of names and the retaining of educational and other records, the actual work of bringing together the congregation seeking a minister and the minister seeking a congregation has been that of the state secretary-minister. Originally elected with a coterie of evangelists to develop the missionary work within the state or area, the state secretary-minister has become, like the pastor, an administrative officer of the church. Much of his time is devoted to congregations regarding local church programs, perhaps chief of which is the selecting of a minister.

Their general procedures do not abridge congregational authority. The state minister comes to the board of elders, or pulpit committee of the church, usually with the names of several ministers the church might consider. He often urges the convening group to ask the congregation also to submit the names of ministers in whom they may be interested. After this larger list of names has been compiled, "information schedules" with references, educational qualifications, and the record of each minister under consideration are obtained. After these records are reviewed, the custom is to narrow the list to three or four. Additional consultations are held, before the elders, or pulpit committee begins to check the references in the fields where those under consideration now work, or have worked. Often the committee visits the field and hears the prospective pastor from his own pulpit before they recommend to the board or congregation.

The Pension Fund, was launched in 1895 as a Board of Ministerial Relief to face the growing problem of lifetime support for Disciple ministers. I shall not recite its full history here, as it is documented elsewhere.[21] It began as a committee on ministerial support and relief of the general convention in 1873, followed by its formal organization by a group of laymen as the Board of Ministerial Relief in 1895. It introduced a reserve Pension Plan in 1915 which was in full operation by 1919. In 1928, came the organization of the Pension Fund with that name but under the same charter of the Board of Ministerial Relief. From its beginning a steady effort has been put forth by the Pension Fund, particularly appealing to elders, deacons, board chairmen, pulpit and finance committees, to take a hard and steady look at ministerial support based upon 1 Corinthians 9:14, that they that "preach the Gospel" should expect their "living of the Gospel." The Fund has pointed out that living days usually exceed preaching days and support needs to be continued into those times when preaching is no longer possible.

The establishment of the *Pension Fund*, I would put as the *fifth* major change for Disciple ministers in this century. The effect of this organization was not merely the introduction of a plan to take care of the widow and the orphan, the disabled minister, or the aged and retired servant of the church. It profoundly influenced the entire matter of ministerial support. In 1925, Disciples ranked tenth among Protestant churches in average salaries for its ministers. By 1963, the National Council study revealed that Disciples had moved to third. What is more significant than rank is that in 1925, when the average salary was less than $2,300 annually, there were almost as many ministers receiving $10,000 a year or more as in 1963 when the average salary was near $6,000. Thus the standard of support has moved up more rapidly from the bottom than from the top. All in all a much more wholesome attitude has developed in regard to the entire matter of ministerial support, but there are still far too many congregations without pastors because they cannot support one, and ministers still try to meet current bills on less than adequate support.

The *sixth* matter that changed concepts in the twentieth century for the ministry of Disciples has been the *ecumenical influences*. Among these, has been that of the military chaplaincy. At the height of World War II, over seven hundred Disciples ministers were chaplains. Since then, both in the Korean and Vietnam conflicts, the number has passed the one hundred mark several times. The overwhelming majority of these ministers have not been career chaplains. They serve but a few years in the military and return to serve the church in various capacities. No one can pass through this practical ecumenical experience unaffected.

On every front today it is obvious that we cannot isolate ourselves as we once did along the American frontier, while giving "lip service" to Christian unity.

There are today the theological conversations into which many pastors have entered in local communities and abroad. Because of commitment to Christian unity, Disciple ministers try to find common ground upon which they can stand with others.

They lead in local Councils of Churches, as well as other ecumenical enterprises. And there are many today, who, though encouraged by the ecumenical conversations, will take more heart when they see more mutuality of action at the community level in which they work. Generally, our folk expect their minister to participate in both ecumenical enterprises and interfaith undertakings. In fact, many will take the leadership in these matters if their preacher will not.

Though not often mentioned in *Midstream*, for Disciples, ecumenicity also takes on its varied and day-by-day practical forms. A Methodist, a Baptist and a Presbyterian church are nearer my home than the congregation of which I am a member. Every month or so, when I am home and have an opportunity to get acquainted, I discover another neighbor who was formerly a Disciple and who now attends one of the three nearer churches. The pastors of these churches tell me that former Disciples are among their best leaders. This story can be duplicated in every corner of the land. Ecumenicity comes easily for Disciples. After proposing an old motto for this spirit, that of "sinking into oblivion", I have concluded that a much better one is "we would rather switch than fight."

It is not often that Disciple ministers immediately follow their ex-members, since most denominations will accept our members without re-orientation, but not our preachers. Nevertheless, we seem to contribute ministers to the "greater needs" of the United Church of Christ, the Presbyterians and the Episcopalians. We "break even" in swaps with the Methodists, but take from the Churches of Christ, the Baptists, the Church of God and some other groups. All in all, Disciples now give more than they receive in this ecumenical exchange. And that, too, is a switch from the last century.

It should be noted that not all this pretended practical ecumenicity is good. There has been a drift toward lack of commitment and involvement on the part of many urbanized people today, who do not find themselves settled in the *koinonia* of any congregation and, hence, are unrelated to the ministry of the church. More and more, people are making their choice of religious faith and of a particular congregation, not upon theological concepts, but upon the basis of political, social and economic factors. The minister today faces all the frustrations that come out of this.

Samuel Blizzard put it succinctly, by saying:

The roles a minister performs in present day American society are basically equivocal. On the one hand, the Church has a traditional set of norms by which he is expected to be guided. On the other hand, the parishioner has a set of functional expectations by which the minister's professional service is judged. This is the minister's dilemma.[22]

Accompanying this is a rising concern, which is almost a hostility with seminary students, but exists also with others as well, who seem to be reluctant to accept this dilemma and to love the pastoral ministry as they ought.

One seminary authority has said:

The question which hangs in the air over seminary talk about this Christ-Culture dilemma is "can the church be reformed before too much disillusionment sets in," or "before a sizeable minority of the seminarians back entirely away from the ordained ministries."[23]

He adds,

One must say that the discontent of the younger group is close to real disloyalty, not in the sense of apostasy, but as a complete disavowal of almost everything which is conventionally 'churchy'. This critical group of seminarians is muttering, "Let's chuck it and look for something entirely different in the way of Christian Community; and, if we can't find it or create it, let's crawl back into the landscape of laity, not as clergy."[24]

The proposed alternatives are not too clear, or specific, nor do they accomplish much but credit to some rather old ideas the terms of "new" or "experimental ministries." For

Disciples, coffee house encounters are about as new as informal groups around a frontier campfire and that is saying something in their favor, which I intend. Indeed, the Christian ministry and the church must ever go where people are—and that is not always a geographic matter. Members of the Campbell-Stone Movement should be willing to abandon all formalism and institutionalism if that move can be shown to be essential to the coming of the Kingdom.

It is possible that the crisis in the ministry has been exaggerated by a modern press wanting to accept only the extraordinary and hence to write up the dissatisfactions and frustrations of a very few ministers. On the other hand, some problems cannot be easily dismissed.

In the course of the past year I have made a special effort to note the general expressions of concern of our ministers. Among these are: (1) Pastors would like to be considered as ministers of more than the local church. They expect to be a part of a broadening, more inclusive and ecumenical relationship. (2) They express the desire for a way to be found in which both they, and their spouses, can have more intimate relationships with the local congregation. If this cannot be attained, they are anxious to find some method in which they can secure identification with a small group of Christians to experience a more personal sense of fellowship. (3) They confess need for renewal and re-education. (4) They hope for recognition as a part of the professional staff of the whole church and are willing to be measured by its standards. (5) They would like to find more adequate and fair ways of placement and support.

In their search for relatedness, responsibility and renewal, ministers confess that, if such comes to the church, it will likely begin with themselves. Ministers acknowledge failure to translate the theory of the gospel into action in the current, complicated urban situation. They recognize the need for becoming an equipping ministry for their congregations and that there should be more inter-action in the communication of the gospel. They express a need to develop in their ministries a deepened concern for the individual. They recognize that they must become teachers in an institution of learners. They understand that their role as chief administrator in the church is not just a matter of having a smooth running organization, but of equipping other persons to fulfill their individual ministries. All along the line the emphasis is upon action, which is typical of Disciples. They are even skeptical of themselves, of becoming simply voices of prophecy in which there is no participation. They know that the church *is* ministry, and that this ministry *is given* by Jesus Christ.

Yet, not one would say his public ministry is altogether a joyous or easy one. I find ministers always in a struggle. Like any other Christian, spiritual birth is painful, and one goes clear through this life just trying to be born! When the preacher is young and in school, he usually feels overwhelmed by this. When he begins to think he has experience, along comes someone and tells him that all the old assumptions are wrong. When he is old, he is called upon to make the greatest adjustment of all, that of retiring. Even when he dies, he is scarcely allowed the privacy of meeting his maker, as all gather 'round and take measurement of his faith.

Today many seminary students cry, "relevance", and the temptation for the older generation is to shout back, "responsibility." The fact is that the church cannot exist unless it is in constant renewal with God and ever relating itself to humanity where, and as, it is. At the same time, there is the heavy responsibility of pressing on toward the goal of the high calling, given us by our Lord, and made all the more sacred by the fact that "a great cloud of witnesses," the living and those separated by the one-way glass of death, look on expectantly. These are they whose devotion has accorded them every right to anticipate nothing but the best in our personal ministries.

Over against this remain vestiges of the "hired man" viewpoint and many a pastor needs to be relieved from some of the mimeographing, fund raising and public praying he does; in order to become a teacher of teachers, a counselor of counselors and a Christian with Christians.

Such renewal cannot be effected in the church by the minister alone and without the intended cooperation of many. As one observes, "Our problem is this: We have enough good men who are fit for the ministry, but we do not have a ministry that is fit for our best men."[25] And while I am sure that many good persons will protest this statement, it is none the less true. It is the recurrent fact of finding it impossible to minister *apart from* the ministry of the church. While it is true that ministers are most given to the twin sins of pride and despair, it is not possible even for a Paul to be fruitful in an unconcerned and self-assured Athens. There must be a fellowship.

The fact is that a lack of fellowship and support in the proclamation of the Gospel continues to be the number one enemy of the effectiveness of the church in fulfilling its mission. The minister who would be effective in today's complex society *must* be an equipping minister. And the *only* way of his achieving this is *by being a part of a concerned fellowship.* His congregation may completely change within a matter of a few years or a few months. There is no such a thing as an established church in an established community anymore. So the pastor must function quickly as a catalyst, much as did the early Apostles, or he will soon find himself preaching the Gospel only to himself or justifying himself in being in some social service. On the other hand, if he is an effective teacher and an equipping minister, the word will get around and greater responses will be forthcoming. If he supplements this by living the kind of life—that visible rhetoric—which demonstrates that "he *is* a man of truth, he will find, I feel confident, that he is a part of a growing fellowship in Jesus Christ."[26]

Of course, if there were sufficiently committed Christians, the ranks of the ministry would always be full. Individuals would vie for the opportunity of serving the Lord, if they really held Him to be such. But, as W. T. Moore observed many years ago, "It is simply impossible to make an effective minister of the gospel out of one of these purely professional Christians."[27] An individual who is not spiritually inclined, who has no intimate relationship with the Master, cannot under his own power draw people more closely to God.

Never have we needed ministers more than right now. Congregations are without pastors and scores of people never hear the good news. For several years, some churches of the Campbell-Stone Movement, with its historic appeal to clarity, reason and thoughtfulness, have been tempted to compromise for an uneducated, partially-trained ministry, that is, for one able to fill what seemed to be "vacant" pulpits and live on less than subsistance, and thus serve small, century-old congregations. As a matter of fact, since 1900, many Bible Colleges have gotten their start as "preacher plants" because of this prevailing socio-economic situation in rural America. Such colleges can quickly and cheaply furnish a supply. The alternative is to choose higher standards for the ministry. The upholding of such standards in themselves would either necessitate greater activity from such congregations or bring about some form of Christian unity.

I do not believe that we are quite as fearful of the heresy that comes from ignorance as our forefathers, because fewer "shortcuts" are advocated in education, and less compromise of standards offered, in order to have "filled pulpits." At the same time, we are often ensnared on the other "horn." We are in the position of having developed a number of ministers who find it increasingly difficult to communicate with ingrown rural congregations. This is not due, however, to being "over-educated." The basic problem is a matter of support, and a lack of commonality in regard to the mission of the church and its ministry.

Many Disciples like to think we have a professional ministry (in the highest and best sense of that word) with high standards accepted primarily out of personal commitment. We do not. We have good men and women in spite of this lack. Many do not really know what a profession is. They are so sports oriented, they equate it with "playing for pay." But a real profession is distinguished by more important considerations. Examine any of the learned professions and the things that mark them as such are that they require moral standards, educational achievement, a centrally recognized system of admission to their ranks, the continual upgrading of abilities and standards, a method of exclusion of the unworthy, and the recognition of achievement within the group. Law, medicine, teaching and nursing all qualify in these regards. But as for the ministry, particularily in the Campbell-Stone Movement, there has been little desire to move toward fulfillment of such requirements. The fact that in this way we have made this calling something lower than any other honorable profession, and the lack of support that we have given it, has created an instability in the pastoral ministry which should concern us all. It is true that much of this may be the minister's fault, but I cannot help but believe that some fault lies in the absence of a Christian system.

We permit listing in the Year Book each year more than two thousand persons who do not regularly serve in any church vocation. To the outside world, this listing constitutes "ministerial standing" and the individual who wishes to trade upon it can easily do so and find support in the looseness of our Disciple structures. This is the reason that in one week's time the daily press could report ministers of the

Campbell-Stone Movement holding a seance for a prominent bishop or learning to scuba dive in order to marry a couple under water.

If these were the last words for our ministry they would be dismal, indeed, but they are neither the first nor the last. When one sees those presently who serve unstintingly, and recalls those who brought this Movement its glories, we take heart. So, we do not weep over our history or remain without hope for the present or the future. For those who despair of the future are often those who also have remorse for the past, since they must look backward with regret, they can only look forward with fear.

Much more needs to be said concerning the mutual ministry and the set-apart ministry. Basically it is this: It is always bad to make religion professional, but it is not bad, but commendable, to make the pastor a professional. To be such an equipping minister requires skill and knowledge and sensitivity in order to develop the mutual ministry of the church.

At no time has this kind of equipping, functional ministry been more sorely needed than now, and nowhere is it more clearly described than in Ephesians 4:11-12. The New English Bible translates this section:

"And these were His gifts: some to be apostles, some prophets, some evangelists, some pastors and teachers, to equip God's people for work in His service to the building up of the body of Christ."[28]

This is the purpose of order and office in the church as Campbell contended, and upon which the anatomical analogies of the Apostle rest, as he describes the church. The *whole* church is called in ministry. But this does *not* mean there is a lesser place for the person in the set apart public ministry. The editor of *The Christian* approached it right the other day when he wrote:

When we speak and write of the minister today someone is sure to say that the minister is no better than anyone else

—thus missing the point of the discussion. Or, another person may stress the place of the elders in the church to the point where it appears that the ordained serves in some kind of a secondary ministry.

For what it is worth, we offer the observation that far more than half of the Disciples look upon the minister and his office in a somewhat different way than they look upon themselves as members of the congregation. This difference is not based entirely upon the minister's technical studies and competence. In fact, there are often members of the congregation who may not have the same degrees but who have equal or superior insights into truth. However much we may theorize about our mutual ministry, those of us in the pews are quite satisfied there is also an order of the ministry.[29]

From our beginnings I believe that we have enjoyed the blessings of an Almighty God who has provided us a dedicated ministry, humble before Him, but proud to serve as ministers. Thomas Campbell probably led the way in this. He wanted to be called nothing more than a minister of Christ. He appended to his signature VDM, *Verbi Divini Minister*—a minister of the Word of God.[30]

Ministers today may share this same pride and humility, when they recognize themselves to be simply what the name implies, and that is, *servant*. They are followers of the suffering servant who came not to be ministered unto but to minister. They may regard themselves as prophets when they proclaim fearlessly, but always lovingly, the Word of God to a pagan and perverse generation. They can know themselves to be priests, not in the withdrawn sense, but in the intercessory sense of representing people in public worship before God, a priest among priests. They can know themselves to be elders, not autocrats, by having the maturity to rule well and administer the affairs of the church with other elders. They may see themselves as ambassadors who represent the King of Kings. And many of them know themselves, whether with or without the title, as pastors who care for the sheep as does the good shepherd. All of these things they may take to be a part of their ministry without pretense, ministering simply in the name of the Lord, and not in their own. They know that they are servants bound to no man, often without rightful "hire", yet not "for sale" or "to be bought" by men, having been redeemed by the one Lord they serve. They recognize, perhaps more than any other generation, that if they are to be servants, they must be self-forgetting, willing to pour themselves into these genuine ministerial roles.

One fine day an ordination was held in Bethany, West Virginia, over a hundred years ago. It was that of C. L. Loos. After the elders of the local congregation and of neighboring congregations as well had participated and had testified both to the character and qualifications of the candidate, who they said, had demonstrated his "ability to labor both in word and in doctrine",[31] the congregation participated in a prayer response to the charge, which should be ours today. It was:

> "Go with Thy servant, Lord,
>   His every step attend;
> All needful help to him afford
>   And bless him to the end."

NOTES

1. Jack Meyer, Sr., *The Preacher and His Work*, Revised and enlarged edition (Athens, Alabama: C.E.I. Publishing Co., 1960).

2. Dudley Strain, *The Measure of a Minister* (St. Louis: The Bethany Press, 1964).

3. Jack Meyer, Sr., *The Preacher and His Work*, p. 110.

4. F. D. Kershner, *The Restoration Handbook* (Cincinnati: Standard Publishing Company, 1918), Part IV, Lesson 5, p. 26.

5. *Yearbook of Christian Churches (Disciples of Christ)* (Indianapolis: International Convention of Christian Churches, 1966), p. m-l.

6. Unpublished studies of The Commission of the Ministry (Indianapolis: Pension Fund of Christian Churches, 1928), pp. 10-24.

7. *Ibid.*, p. 44.

8. W. M. Smith, "Polling the Congregation for A Preacher," *The Christian* (June 26, 1966), p. 806.

9. Charles T. Hudson, W. L. McEver and Manford Pigg, "A Study in the Supply and Demand of the Ministry of Disciples of Christ" (unpublished B. D. Thesis, Phillips University, 1944), and Robert K. Ordway, "A Study of Tenure of Ministers Among Disciples of Christ" (unpublished B. D. Thesis, Christian Theological Seminary, 1959).

10. My own current studies based upon withdrawal from Pension Plan, specific requests for withdrawal from ministerial lists both of the Pension Fund and of Christian Churches and The Yearbook of Disciples of Christ, with individual references compiled from 1960 to date. Study will be completed in 1970.

11. T. J. Mullen, *The Renewal of the Ministry* (Nashville: Abingdon Press, 1963), p. 110.

12. M. E. Boring, "Ichabod . . . 'the Glory Has Departed,'" *The Christian* (October 8, 1967), p. 1286.

13. Based on an analysis of Madison Evans', *Biographical Sketches of Pioneer Preachers in Indiana* (Philadelphia; J. Challen & Sons, 1862).

14. A. R. Sharp, "The Shortage of the Ministry," *The Christian* (October 8, 1967), Vol. 105, p. 1288.

15. F. E. Davison, "The Ordaining of a Minister," *The Christian-Evangelist*, Vol. 74 (Feb. 13, 1936), pp. 213-214.

16. R. E. Osborn, *In Christ's Place—Christian Ministry in Today's World* (St. Louis: The Bethany Press, 1967), p. 226.

17. *Ibid*, p. 227.

18. Atlanta Declaration Committee, "Where Are We Going in Restructure," a pamphlet published in 1967, item 4.

19. B. A. Hunter, "But Why Ordination?", *The Christian-Evangelist* (March 19, 1936), p. 377.

20. R. E. Osborn, *In Christ's Place—Christian Ministry in Today's World*, p. 67.

21. See: W. M. Smith, *For the Support of the Ministry* (Indianapolis: Pension Fund of Disciples of Christ, 1956), 240 pages.

22. S. G. Blizzard, "The Minister's Dilemma," *The Christian Century*, Vol. 73 (April 25, 1956), p. 509.

23. W. G. Wagoner, *Bachelor of Divinity* (New York: Association Press, 1963), pp. 22, 23.

24. *Ibid*, p. 27.

25. T. J. Mullen, *The Renewal of the Ministry*, p. 35.

26. *Ibid*, p. 63.

27. W. T. Moore, *Preacher Problems* (New York: Fleming H. Revell Co., 1907), Second edition, p. 9.

28. Ephesians 4:11-12, *The New English Bible* (New York: Oxford University Press, 1961).

29. H. E. Short, "Defining the Ministry," an editorial, *The Christian* (October 8, 1967), p. 1290.

30. L. G. McAllister, *Thomas Campbell—Man of the Book* (St. Louis: Bethany Press, 1954), p. 147.

31. M. M. Davis, *The Eldership* (Cincinnati: Standard Publishing Company, 1912), pp. 52-53.